Jersey'
German Tu...

Text
Michael Ginns, M.B.E.

Tunnel Plans
Paul Burnal

Production
Dave Williams

Editor
Matthew Costard, B.A. (Hons)

Published by:
Channel Islands Occupation Society (Jersey) Limited,
3 Newcastle Close,
La Grande Route de St. Jean,
St. John,
JERSEY
Channel Islands
JE3 4FZ

ISBN 978-0-9550086-1-0

Contents

All photographs are by the author unless otherwise stated.

Foreword

It is now nearly twenty years since *German Tunnels in the Channel Islands* was published, and so popular did it prove that all copies were sold within a short space of time. There have been incessant calls for a second edition to appear.

As its title suggests, this second edition focuses on Jersey alone, and the tunnels in the other islands of Guernsey, Alderney and Sark will now be covered in a separate publication produced by Festung Guernsey.

Much of the original text remains, but, where appropriate, it has been revised and updated, and the opportunity has been taken to include new material. The format of the book has also been improved, and the tunnel plans are now in colour, along with the majority of the photographs and other illustrations.

The tunnels themselves have changed little during the intervening period, although some have been more effectively sealed and are now completely inaccessible. The mushroom farm in *Ho 1* is no longer operating, but much of the complex remains in commercial use as a dry storage facility. The German Military Underground Hospital has been renamed the 'Jersey War Tunnels' and has undergone a number of changes in order to keep pace with visitor expectations, but it remains one of Jersey's top tourist attractions and will doubtless be so for many years to come.

Michael Ginns, MBE

August, 2012

1. Introduction

"... there must be ample accommodation for stores and ammunition, for mobile diversion parties, and for armoured cars ..."

These words, which were encapsulated in Hitler's famous Directive of 20th October 1941, set the seal of approval on a series of tunnelling projects which had begun several weeks previously, and which still have repercussions today.

Of all the building activities in which the occupying German Forces engaged themselves in the Channel Islands between 1941 and 1945, none has captured the public imagination more than the tunnels which were driven into the sides of the Islands' lovely valleys.

Despite the passage of time, interest in the tunnels does not wane but, if anything, continues to increase. This lies not so much in the fact that the tunnels are just tunnels, but because they are *German* tunnels. Thus, they must, according to popular belief, have some sinister purpose, and over the years they have given rise to more speculation than any other wartime construction project in the Channel Islands.

This has ranged from the ridiculous (that the tunnels were to form the basis of an underground railway system), to the hysterical (that they were to house gas chambers to exterminate the civilian population). In 1972 one self-professed 'expert' turned up claiming to have seen the original 'secret' plans which showed that the tunnels were to be used to launch V2 rockets against England!

However, any dedicated researcher or historian will quickly find that the genuine and original wartime maps showing the precise location and purpose of the tunnels are readily available from several archive sources. These clearly show that they were, as ordered by Hitler, intended to provide secure underground shelter for food, fuel and ammunition, as well as reserve troops and vehicles. These maps are included in *Verstärkung der Kanalinseln 1941* (Reinforcing the Channel Islands 1941) which is included in microfilm publication T 78 317, available from the National Archives & Records Service, Washington, USA (Frame Nos. 271647 *et seq*).

British National Archives (NA) document WO 2090A 55851 also shows that in 1944 British Intelligence was well aware of the existence of the tunnels and had noted that they were intended purely for storage purposes and were not built to any particular alignment – which would have been the case had they been intended to launch flying bombs.

The German language provides two words, '*Tunnel*' and '*Stollen*', which mean 'tunnel', but the surviving records show that in the parlance of the German Fortress Engineers, the Channel Islands' tunnels were always referred to as '*Hohlgangsanlagen*', or 'cave-passage-installations' (abbreviated to '*Ho*'), and 'cave' is a very apt description for the unlined sections of the German excavations, as anyone who has seen them will readily agree.

Buried deep in the surrounding hillsides beneath anything up to 110 feet (36 metres) of rock, the German tunnels would have been proof against even the heaviest and most prolonged shelling or aerial bombardment. Virtually undetectable from the air, most had at least two adits which, in conjunction with the semi-circular plan layout used in most cases for the primary galleries, allowed vehicle convoys unimpeded circulation.

It was in Jersey that the idea of tunnelling was first conceived and where most was achieved; the plan was extended to the other Islands but, due to the shortage of the necessary manpower and equipment occasioned by the construction of the heavy coastal artillery battery *Mirus* in Guernsey, the 29 known tunnels planned for that island, as well as the nine for Alderney, never attained the standard of those in Jersey. In any case, serious work on the tunnels came to a virtual standstill when the construction crews were recalled to the Continent to work on the main 'Atlantic Wall' in October, 1943.

Ownership of the tunnels today is vested in whoever owns the land above, as decreed by old Channel Islands' laws which, without going into too fine detail, provide that any landowner has title to whatever lies beneath his/her property down to the centre of the Earth. Insofar as the German tunnels are concerned, this has on occasions been a vexatious point, and has even led to a court case (see *Ho 8*).

The purpose of this book is to answer the many queries which people still have about the tunnels; to eliminate (hopefully!) the endless stream of ridiculous myths and legends that they engender; and to correct the belief of many visitors to Jersey who say "Your island must make a mint out of those War Tunnels". It would be nice to think that this book could be a definitive work on the subject, but this can never be the case without access to the original German tunnel plans. That these will ever be found is a forlorn hope as it can be said, without fear of contradiction, that all the detailed plans of the German Fortress Engineers and the *Organisation Todt*, for the fortification of the Channel Islands, were destroyed well before the end of the war.

Nevertheless, certain documents have survived, as detailed below:–

Sources & Acknowledgements

In addition to those sources mentioned above, details of tunnel locations and intended purposes can be found in the *Baufortschrittsmeldunge* (Building Progress Reports) submitted monthly by the respective Fortress Engineers Headquarters in Guernsey and Jersey to *OKW* (*Oberkommando der Wehrmacht* = High Command of the Forces) in Berlin. These reports also give details of the amount of rock removed during excavation and the area of storage space created.

The Progress Reports are complete for the twelve months from May, 1943, to May, 1944, with two examples surviving from May and November, 1942. Entitled *Ausbaubericht der eng. Kanalinseln* (Consolidation Report on the English Channel Islands), they are obtainable from the *Bundesarchiv* (Federal Archives) at Freiburg, Germany, or from the National Archives & Records Service, Washington, USA, on Microfilm Publication T78-317, frame No. 271644 *et seq*.

The post-war account of his wartime command as *Befehlshaber der britische Kanalinseln* (Commander of the British Channel Islands) by *Generalleutnant* Rudolf Graf von Schmettow, entitled *The Channel Islands - Preparations for the Defence against the Invasion, and during the Invasion, until the Surrender,* contains useful tunnel information and is also available from the National Archives, Washington, as their document MS B-833.

Documents which are held at the National Archives (NA), Kew, are quoted by permission of the Controller of HM Stationery Office and are Crown Copyright.

The indefatigable Leslie Sinel's *Occupation Diary* provides useful start dates for certain tunnels, as well as the dates of some accidents therein. Following the tragedy in *Ho 2* in 1962 (see pages 35-38), all the accessible tunnels (except *Ho 5, 8* and *19*, which were in daily usage) were visited and inspected by experts of the British Army (see Appendix V), who drew up plans of the installations concerned. Copies of these plans are held at the States of Jersey Department of the Environment and were made available to the Channel Islands Occupation Society (Jersey) by kind permission of the late Bob Paton when he was Director of Planning.

A word of warning, however! These plans, which cover tunnels *Ho 1, 2, 4, 10, 13* and *15*, are not entirely accurate as, for ease of compilation, all curves have been eliminated and replaced by a series of sharp angles which are totally incorrect. As seen in this book, these plans have been corrected by Paul Burnal wherever he has been able to inspect the tunnels' interiors.

Michael Long and Neil Walker of the States of Jersey Emergency Planning Office kindly provided copies of the 1962 Tunnel Report, and gave us permission to reproduce some of that material with accompanying photographs.

By kind permission of the author and publisher, Ralph Ellington, I have quoted extensively from his very useful little book entitled simply *The German Underground Hospital*. For many years Ralph was proprietor of the café-cum-gift shop which stood in the car park of the then German Military Underground Hospital (now renamed the Jersey War Tunnels) and to which most people headed once they had emerged from the tunnel complex, one of Jersey's leading tourist attractions. Ralph produced his booklet in an attempt to answer the many queries which were put to him over a long period. He had come to realise that these queries were, in the main, identical and centred upon (i) who built the tunnels? (ii) what were the working conditions like? and (iii) why was a hospital put underground? *The German Underground Hospital* was a remarkably honest and objective publication and told the bare truth that many do not like to hear; for example, that the workforce was not all Russian slave labour, but included local people working voluntarily and for high rates of pay. Ralph managed to track down some of these locals and from them gathered much useful information on the working conditions and methods of construction which have been of great use in the compilation of this book.

Fig. 1 - Tunnels for which no plans existed had to be surveyed carefully. Here, inside *Ho19* at La Folie, Wally Dauny holds one end of the tape measure, while Josephine provides the illumination and Paul Burnal does his calculations.

Many other people in Jersey have been most helpful and I would particularly like to thank the following:– Mr. D.J. Huelin for allowing the Occupation Society to visit his land in Beaumont Valley for a talk on the tunnels *Ho 13* and *Ho 15*; the staff and management of Jersey Mushroom Growers Ltd. (operating when my research was first published in *German Tunnels in the Channel Islands* in 1993, but sadly no longer in business), Mr. Steve Liron and Mr. R. Burrows, for permission to explore and photograph, respectively, the interiors of *Ho 1*, *2*, and *Mole Verclut*; Tony Beaumont of the States of Jersey Public Services Department (now the Transport and Technical Services Department), for permitting access to *Ho 5* and *Ho 19*; Stewart Logan, TTS Surveyor, for providing an updated plan of *Ho 19*; Mr. Paul Simmonds of Sanctuary Inns Ltd., for permission to photograph inside the Jersey War Tunnels, and especially the late Joe Mière, former Curator, for his interest and assistance over many years, and his successor, Mr. Jim McScowan.

Mr. Ken Le Montais permitted unlimited access to *Ho Etacquerel* at St. Ouen; Mr. John Hobbs, the former managing director of Jersey Water, and his successor, Mr. Howard Snowden, kindly allowed us to inspect the interior of *Ho 4* in Grands Vaux, our most recent visit being arranged with the assistance of Jersey Water's Mr. Paul Batho.

Mrs. Margaret Long, a prominent member of La Société Jersiaise and the National Trust for Jersey, provided valuable information on tunnelling activities in Beaumont Valley, this being contained in the diary of her late father, Mr. John Cutler Vincent, extracts of which she kindly made available to us.

The late Dr. Leslie Hill, MA, PhD and MC, translated many German documents, these giving a much clearer insight into many matters concerning the tunnels.

I am grateful to all those who have provided photographs - Tony Pike, Neil Walker, Jimmy Gray,

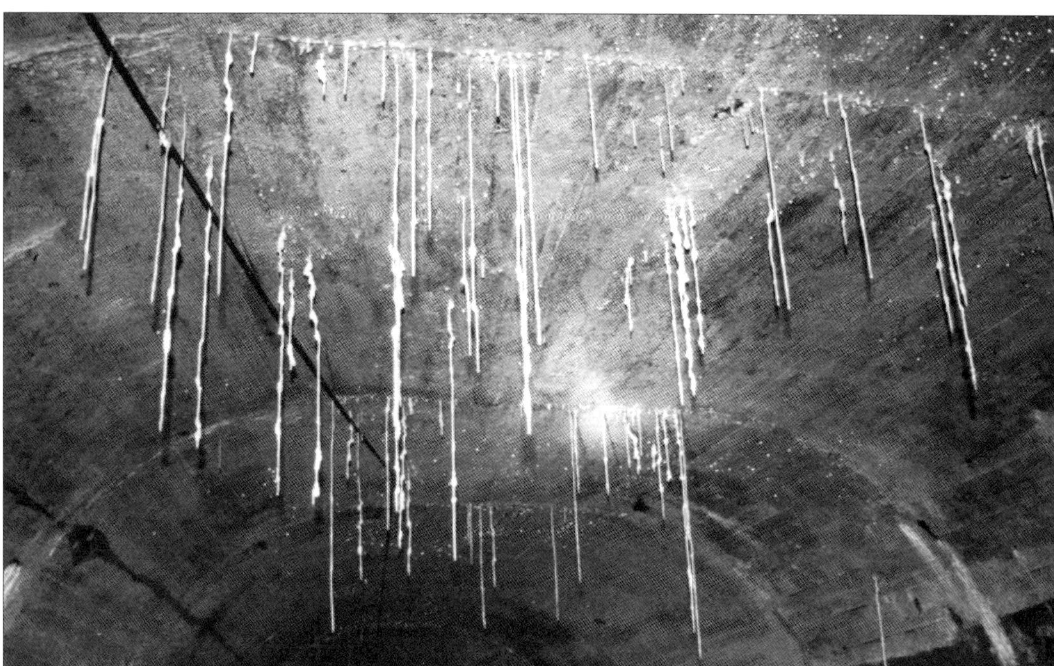

Fig. 2 - Stalactites are common features in tunnels that are not in regular use.

Si Prosser, Steve Powell, Jeremy Hamon, Richard Perchard and Colin Isherwood; and to Maurice Delanoe for allowing us to reproduce his images of *Ho2* .

Finally, my thanks go to the late Robin Cox for his enthusiasm, guidance and information provided, and to Paul Burnal who surveyed and produced the plans of the majority of the tunnels. In order to draw up these plans, it was necessary to explore the many unfinished sections of tunnels; this entailed stumbling over uneven surfaces, braving the uncertainty of rockfalls, and launching ourselves into the uncharted depths of waterlogged sections armed with torches and steel measures. I was always accompanied by my long-suffering wife Josephine and, variously, by Trevor Gouyet or Wally Dauny of the Channel Islands Occupation Society (Jersey).

Michael Ginns, MBE,

August, 2012

2. Surveying & Planning

It is often believed that Hitler's Fortification Directive of 20th October 1941 set in motion the construction programme that was intended to convert the Channel Islands into "impregnable fortresses". Close scrutiny of surviving records, however, shows that this Directive merely confirmed a series of events which first saw the light of day in the early summer of the same year.

When Hitler was first contemplating his attack on the Soviet Union he feared that, once this was launched, Britain would attempt to repossess the Channel Islands as a gesture of support for her new-found ally. To this end, therefore, he ordered that a number of coastal artillery batteries be sent to the Islands to stiffen the defences and this was achieved during the months of March and April, 1941.

The *Führer*, however, soon considered this move to be insufficient, and on 10th June 1941 *OKW* ordered that the defences of the Channel Islands should be increased still further and with immediate effect.

Accordingly, several construction units of the German Army arrived in the Islands and work began on what were known as 'reinforced field type' fortifications (i.e. with reinforced concrete up to one metre in thickness). While this work was in hand, the surveying and planning for the permanent fortifications began with the arrival, in July, 1941, of *Generalmajor* Rudolf Schmetzer, who held a position with the lengthy title of *Inspekteur der Landbefestigung bei Oberbefehlshaber West* (Inspector of Ground Fortifications at Commander-in-Chief West).

Schmetzer set up his Headquarters at Elizabeth College, Guernsey, and was accompanied by *Festungspionierstab 19* (Fortress Engineer Staff 19, and hereinafter referred to by its usual abbreviation of *'Festpistab'*). A *Festpistab* unit normally consisted of a Headquarters and two *Abschnittgruppe* (Sector Groups), in this case designated *I/19* and *II/19*.

To Jersey, and based at the Grand Hotel, went *Festpistab 14* together with *Abschnittgruppe II/14*, but with *I/14* detached to Alderney. All were, as stated, under the direction of Schmetzer. Fortress Engineer units of the German Army consisted of experts in all fields of military engineering and strategy, e.g., camouflage, geology, artillery, reinforced concrete defences and so on. It was the brief of the *Festpistab* units to produce a tactical/technical survey for ultimate submission to *OKW* and final approval by Hitler. This, as already stated, resulted in the Fortification Directive of October, 1941.

The experts of the various *Festpistab* units had to begin from scratch, as the intelligence of the German High Command regarding the topography and geography of the Channel Islands was virtually nil. During the past 65 years or so, various writers/journalists who have visited the Channel Islands and seen the German defences, particularly the Underground Hospital in Jersey (now the Jersey War Tunnels), have ventured the theory that all these massive works must have been planned well before the war with the Channel Islands in mind. This is utter nonsense and it is equally obvious that none of these writers has referred to primary sources.

A detailed examination of contemporary German records shows that until the German Army had captured Paris in June, 1940, the High Command had not given even a moment's consideration to the existence of the Channel Islands, let alone to capturing them; their knowledge of the Islands' defences was also abysmally deficient, a fact that led to the tragic and unnecessary air raids on Guernsey and Jersey on 29th June 1940 (for a detailed account of the air raids on, and the actual occupation of, the Channel Islands, see *Channel Islands Occupation Review No. 18*, pp. 62-79).

Insofar as the origins of the tunnels are concerned, the High Command of the Army (*OKH*) was well aware that, should the Islands be attacked, a siege situation might well arise and it was therefore imperative that large quantities of essential supplies (e.g. food, fuel and ammunition) should be stockpiled in stores that were both bomb and shell proof. For the time being, old 19th Century fortifications were utilised as their massive granite construction suited them, almost ideally, for the role of shelters. Thus, for example, Fort George in Guernsey became a vast ammunition dump, while Fort Regent in Jersey housed petrol. Doubtless, in Alderney, Fort Albert was utilised.

However, these old fortifications were not always best located for storage purposes, being too centralised, and it was desirable that supplies should be distributed equally over each island so that if a landing should be successful, not everything would fall into enemy hands at once.

The first definite mention of tunnels is contained in a report dated 26th June 1941, entitled 'Comments on the Present State of the Fortifications on the British Channel Islands'. Paragraph 2(v) of this document states that "... the Fortress Engineers, together with the construction units, will be employed in the excavation of underground installations for communications centres and the stockpiling of all sorts of goods." (see *Verstärkung der Kanalinseln*, CIOS *Archive Book No. 3*, page 8).

Fig. 3 - Early days of the Occupation, and drums of petrol are delivered to the fuel dump at Fort Regent. *Author's Collection*

Little would have been known of the surveying and excavation of the Jersey tunnels had it not been for Professor Walther Klüpfel, an eminent geologist and lecturer at the University of Giessen in Germany. A soldier in the First World War, Klüpfel was recalled for military service in 1941 and given the rank of *Oberleutnant*. After a brief period of military training, the Professor was posted to a mapping unit of the 319 Infantry Division at Granville. Soon, however, his professional expertise in geology was in demand and he was posted to *Festpistab 14* on 27th July 1941, and took up residence at the Grand Hotel.

Fortunately, for posterity, Professor Klüpfel committed all his activities to his diary which, following his death, eventually came to the attention of Dr. A.C. Bishop and Dr. E. Launert of the Department of Mineralogy at the British Museum; using Klüpfel's notes, they produced a most informative article entitled 'A Wehrmacht Geologist in Jersey' which appeared in the *Channel Islands Occupation Review, 1979* (pp. 30-37). This article alone gives an insight into the enormous amount of study that went into the planning and surveying of the Jersey tunnels, as well as other preparatory work associated with the creation of 'Fortress Jersey'.

Reproduced below is a synopsis of the 1979 article insofar as it applied to tunnels:-

Tunnels

Of all the construction works, the storage tunnels seem most to capture the popular imagination. The military requirement was for there to be ample accommodation for stores, mobile diversion parties and armoured cars and it was soon realised that such provision could be made by tunnelling into the valley sides.

The decision to drive tunnels was taken before Klüpfel's arrival in Jersey in August, 1941, and at least some had been sited before then, for as early as 10th September 1941, he gives details of a visit to the St. Peter's Valley area mentioning Tesson Mill, Victoria Inn, and Panigot. Written in ink beside these pencil entries in his field notebook are the words "house above Victoria tunnel", and, if it is assumed that the entry in ink is contemporary with the pencilled field notes and not a later addition – it was probably made when he was making a transcription of his field notes - the Victoria tunnel (Hohlgangsanlage 1) was then under construction. The initial work was undertaken by the Reichsarbeitsdienst, whose badge is preserved over the portal of Ho 1, before the arrival of the main force of the OT workers in December, 1941. From the entries in Klüpfel's notes it seems likely that work was also under way on Ho 2 and Ho 8 as well. Incidentally, only rarely does Klüpfel refer to the tunnels by their 'official' designations; to him Ho 1 is 'Victoria Stollen' and Ho 8 is 'Emphrie Stollen'. Never are the functions of the tunnels mentioned and never is the word 'hospital' mentioned in connection with Ho 8. Although he visited virtually every tunnel, it was Ho 1 and Ho 8 that were to occupy most of his time.

The speed with which the tunnelling got underway can be judged by his mention of the Doktorhaus tunnel (Mont Matthieu, St. Ouen) on 11th September 1941, and in early January, 1942, he records visits to Bellozanne Valley and, with Major May, to the St. Aubin's tunnel (Ho 5). A rock profile is recorded of Ho 2 at this time and he refers also to a tunnel on Jubilee Hill. The Grands Vaux complex of tunnels is first mentioned in the Spring of 1942 when, on 16th March, he went with Oberstleutnant Eimler and Hauptmann Lange to visit a tunnel (Ho 12) at Ponterrin Mill which he states was being driven "on west side of quarry". By June of 1942 it was possible to identify Ho 10 as the tunnel being driven from Mal Assis quarry and, on 13th August, he mentions "upper tunnel, Paul Mill", which is probably Ho 4 or Ho 11.

Regular visits were made to the tunnels and on 20th January 1943, he gives a list of firms being employed, or being considered for employment, to sink boreholes. One of these firms, Odrich of Rohrbach-bei-Landau, he noted, also drove tunnels. At about this time no less a person than the Military Commander, Generalmajor Graf von Schmettow, visited Ho 5 at St. Aubin. The tunnel Ho 13, Beaumont Valley, Munition Store IV, was under construction by 26th January 1943, and the Etacquerel tunnel is mentioned on 3rd March.

February and March were busy months for Klüpfel for he made eight visits to Ho 8 alone and on 12th March he drafted a 'short geological report on the Emphrie tunnel area' which summarised the geological conditions in the Ho 8 tunnels and drew attention to an area of disturbed and faulted rock in the western part of the tunnel area. He indicated the ground to the south of the tunnel to be a critical area and predicted that sound, unfaulted rock would be met there. Presumably this refers to a projected, but unbuilt, projection of the tunnel system, for he goes on to mention four projected chambers which, in his view, were well sited, because they would run nearly perpendicular to the bedding of the rock. The strike of the bedding, when unaffected by the faulting, here runs in a direction that varies from E-W to ENE-WSW, and so the four projected chambers must have had a roughly N-S alignment.

The month of August, 1943, was taken up almost entirely with visits to Ho 1, and on 17th August 1943, he drafted, for transmission to Festungspionierstab 19, a 'geological report on the storage tunnel system Ho 1, Jersey'. Three different rock groups were recognised, separated by faults with displacements estimated as being 100 metres or more. A major fault was met in the northern part of the tunnel system and this was correlated with a fault identified at the surface east of Panigot. The fault zone was some 50 metres wide and a projected tunnel and storage chamber lay within the affected area, and so he recommended that the tunnel be diverted to the south and driven in sound rock. To reach a projected area of sound rock north of the fault zone, he further recommended that the most direct route be taken through the zone of broken rock; although Klüpfel mentions a map showing these structures it is unfortunate that no copy has survived the war. The report clearly took some time to complete, for, on 30th August 1943, he wrote "finish Ho 1", and his list of jobs to be done in August included "OT tunnels, 17 wells, sand and gravel, water map". His work involved detailed measurement of the rock structures and it is hoped to publish the result of his work elsewhere. It is most interesting that nowhere does Klüpfel mention that he encountered dykes of igneous rock in the tunnels, though several are recorded by Dr. A.E. Mourant and Dr. A.D. Squire who separately inspected and logged the tunnels after the war. On 26th August 1943, Klüpfel records a visit to the Fort Regent tunnel (Ho 19) and in his later notes there is a reference to Verclut Point, the only clue that he might have visited the tunnel at St. Catherine.

This, however, is jumping ahead somewhat, so we must return to 1941. By the end of the summer of that year the survey for the permanent fortification of the Channel Islands was complete and had been submitted to *OKW* for assessment.

Fig. 4 - *Major* Heider, on the staff of the *Feldkommandantur*, stands at the mouth of an embryonic *Ho 8* in 1942.
Société Jersiaise Photographic Archive, Jersey

On 16th October 1941, a conference was held in Berlin; this was attended by Hitler but chaired by *General* Jacob, who held the position of General of Engineers and Fortifications. The outcome of this conference was the Hitler Directive ordering that the Channel Islands should be converted into "impregnable fortresses", a task which was to be carried out without hindrance or delay, not even by the construction of the main Atlantic Wall on the coastline of Western Europe, from Norway to the Spanish border.

The construction order for the main Atlantic Wall was issued on 15th December 1941, and *Generalmajor* Schmetzer took over the supervision of this enormous project. In the Channel Islands he was replaced by *Oberst* von Marnitz who, together with *Festungspionier Kommandeur XIV* (Fortress Engineer Command XIV) which he commanded, now moved into Elizabeth College to assume overall control of *Festpistab 19*, as well as *Festpistab 14* in Jersey and Alderney, and the permanent fortification of the Channel Islands in which the tunnels were to play an important part.

3. The Workforce

Who was responsible for the excavation of the German tunnels in the Channel Islands?

According to coach drivers and the more lurid guide books, it was "... thousands of Russian slave workers driven to work by *SS* men armed with whips and Alsatian dogs, etc., etc."

Not only is this statement basically incorrect but the truth is far more complicated! Once it became clear that the Channel Islands were to be heavily fortified it was equally obvious that the task would be beyond the resources of the Fortress Engineers alone – as, indeed, had the construction of the West Wall (Siegfried Line) in 1938/39. As early as June, 1941, a memo from *OKH* in Berlin had suggested that the *Organisation Todt* might be called upon to assist.

From the early summer of 1941 various *Festungsbaubattalione* (Fortress Construction Battalions), each with one Mining Company on its strength, began to move in under the aegis of the respective *Festpistab* in each island and, by the autumn, these had been joined by specialist tunnelling units in the shape of *4./Gesteinsbohr Btl. 77* (4th Company of Rock Drilling Battalion 77) in Jersey, less one platoon detached to Alderney, and *4./Gesteinsbohr Btl. 157* in Guernsey.

In addition to the above, there also arrived in Jersey in October, 1941, the following companies of the *RAD* (*Reichsarbeitsdienst* or State Labour Service):– *5/302; 1/305 and 4/353;* while to Guernsey went *2/353* and *3/355*. The *RAD* consisted of 17-18 year-olds who, between the end of their Hitler Youth service and call-up into the Armed Forces proper, served in the *RAD* for 18 months, carrying out such tasks as forestry, road building and, eventually, the construction of fortifications.

The *RAD* in Jersey was certainly involved in the creation of the tunnel *Ho 1* in La Route de l'Aleval, off St. Peter's Valley, where they left their mark in the shape of a fine, carved granite keystone over the central, pedestrian entrance, this bearing the crossed pick and shovel emblem of the Labour Service. Another keystone over the lower entrance displays two crossed hammers and the date 1941-42.

In Jersey the *RAD* was quartered in Victoria College school building, Mont Millais, a fact recorded by Leslie Sinel in his *Occupation Diary* (see entry for 15.10.41), although the youthful pioneers are wrongly identified as belonging to the Hitler Youth. Sinel also records the start date for the St. Peter's Valley tunnels as October, 1941, so all these facts tie in neatly.

Fig. 5 - The 4th Company of Rock Drilling Battalion 77 was the only construction unit to leave its 'trade mark' on any bunker in Jersey. This may be seen at Mont Matthieu, St. Ouen.

There was also local volunteer labour. Commencing in 1940, the Germans had been calling for local labour (with varying degrees of success) to work on extensions to the Airport and, again, in 1941, under the control of the *Marinebaudienststelle* (Naval Construction Office), to build emplacements for coastal artillery batteries at such places as Noirmont Point. However, once the permanent fortification of the Channel Islands became imminent in August of the same year, there arrived in Jersey the well remembered construction firm of Theodore Elsche from Cologne. Until January, 1943, when the firm came under the aegis of the *OT*, Elsche was contracted directly to the *Festpistab*.

Setting up his *Bauburo* (Construction Office) at 'Dijon', Victoria Avenue, Elsche immediately began recruiting local labour and his advertisements I REQUIRE THE FOLLOWING CLASSES OF WORKMEN became a regular feature in the *Evening Post*. Elsche is remembered as being a good employer. He never used slave labour, only local and Continental volunteers; doubtless a similar firm must have been established in Guernsey but, if it was, then history has remained silent on the fact.

NOTICE

For my various undertakings on the Island, I require the following labour :

LANDSCAPE GARDENERS, DIGGERS, STONEBREAKERS, BUILDERS, PLASTERERS, STONEBORERS, MACHINE WORKERS, CARPENTERS, FOREMEN.

HOURLY RATE OF PAY FOR WORKERS, 1s. 1d., EXPERTS, 1s. 5d.

FREE CONVEYANCE BETWEEN ST. HELIER AND ESTATE.
THE BUSES WILL STOP ALSO IN ST. AUBIN.

Apply from 8-12 or 2-6, at my Office at Dijon House, in Victoria Avenue.

Applicants must bring their Insurance Cards.

THEODORE ELSCHE, Building Contractor. Branch, St. Helier.

Fig. 6 - The well-remembered German building contractor, Theodore Elsche, advertises for local labour in the *Evening Post.*

To provide 'pick and shovel' labour for the early work on the Jersey tunnels, particularly *Ho 8*, there arrived in the Island a group of political prisoners from occupied countries including 'half-Jews' and others who had incurred the displeasure of the German authorities. These were closely guarded and housed in a camp at Fort Regent named *Lager Ehrenbreitstein*; their hours of work were long and conditions arduous, but apart from this little seems to be known about them other than the fact that they were returned to France in May, 1942.

Once the extent of fortifying the Channel Islands became apparent to the Fortress Engineers, a final decision was made to call in the *Organisation Todt*. In November, 1941, Dr. Fritz Todt visited the Channel Islands and issued his Construction Order which apportioned the tasks that lay ahead to the various construction agencies. Tunnelling became a major responsibility of the *OT*.

The *Organisation Todt*

The ramifications of the *Organisation Todt* (hereinafter referred to as the '*OT*') have been well described in other publications; it will suffice to say here that this vast construction force had its origins in the workforce gathered together by Dr. Todt in 1933, when he was charged by Hitler with the construction of Germany's pre-war motorway system (see CIOS *Archive Book No.8*).

This workforce, as yet without a name, went on to assist the Fortress Engineers with the construction of the West Wall in 1938; it remained in the fighting zone when war broke out a year later, to carry out repairs to roads, railways and bridges. It was at about this time that the term '*Organisation Todt*' first came into being, and the workforce began to wear redundant Czech Army khaki uniforms in order to denote their by now semi-military status in a combat zone. As the German Army advanced into France following the events of May, 1940, the *OT* followed to continue with the work of repairing railways, etc., and clearing blocked canals.

It was not long before the *OT* was ordered to start work on the cross-Channel coastal artillery batteries in the Pas de Calais area and the submarine pens on the French Atlantic coast - and then came Hitler's order for the fortification of the Channel Islands, followed shortly by the general order for the construction of the main Atlantic Wall, two projects in which the *OT* soon became heavily involved.

wielders of picks and shovels, and now found themselves in positions of some power, that gave the *OT* its bad name. From the few photos that have survived depicting the *OT* in the Channel Islands, it can be seen that they were generally an insalubrious bunch.

Fig. 7 - Some tough looking *OT* overseers at *Lager Brinkforth*, St. Ouen's Bay, pose with the Bishop Mèthode of the Russian Orthodox Church in Paris. The Bishop visited Jersey in March, 1943, to consecrate that part of the Strangers' Cemetery, Westmount, used to inter Russian slave workers.
Société Jersiaise Photographic Archive, Jersey

Now the *OT* mushroomed in both scope and size, aided by the large numbers of civilian contracting firms which had been conscripted by law to swell the workforce. Still wearing their khaki uniforms, the original German skilled workers continued to follow their own trades (surveyors, blacksmiths, welders, carpenters, etc.), while the unskilled workers became the overseers of the large numbers of forced labourers which the *OT* gathered up from all the occupied countries of Europe. It was these overseers, who themselves had once been

Nevertheless, these same overseers worked alongside the foreign labourers, and worked hard, expecting everyone else to do the same. No allowance was made for the fact that their charges were underfed and often in poor health as a result. When a forced labourer failed to come up to scratch, the overseer would often lash out, not with the legendary whip, but with whatever came to hand, be it a pick handle or the flat of a shovel.

The workforce controlled by the *OT* in the

Channel Islands fell into the following categories and, bear in mind, they all worked in the tunnels:-

a) *Voluntary workers*: All over Occupied Europe, the *OT* set up recruiting offices; voluntary employment with the Organisation ensured high rates of pay and heavy workers' rations; it also enabled members of the Resistance to get their hands on fortification plans from which they made copies, forwarding these to England by secret means. Voluntary workers signed work contracts for three, six, nine or twelve months during which time they were entitled to periods of leave.

Thus, under this scheme, there came into the Channel Islands skilled workers and foremen of French, Belgian and Dutch nationality who followed their own trades; most lived in commandeered buildings rather than camps, while some even found private lodgings. This class of worker was most definitely not knocked about by the overseers of the *OT*!

b) *Conscripted workers*: These could also be of French origin, rounded up arbitrarily by the Germans in the streets or cinemas of their home town. However, the bulk of workers in this category consisted of down-at-heel French North Africans, unemployed dock workers for example, supplied to the Germans by the collaborationist French Vichy Government and described in a British Intelligence report as "Pétain's offering to Hitler". Workers in this category lived in specially built camps and were to be found in larger numbers in Guernsey and Alderney than in Jersey. They were badly fed and harshly treated by their overseers. (NA document WO/199 2090A).

c) *Republican Spaniards*: (not all of them were Communists, as is generally believed) who had fled to France when Franco won the Spanish Civil War in 1939, and were interned in camps in that country in conditions that were far from ideal. Traded by the Vichy Government to secure the release of French prisoners-of-war from Germany, the Spaniards first worked on the construction of submarine pens on the French Atlantic coast before approximately 2,000 of them came to the Channel Islands.

Included in their ranks were numbers of skilled tradesmen and the *OT* – being cunning - operated a 'divide-and-rule' policy; any Spaniard willing to perform specialist work was offered better conditions. Possibly because they were not all Communists in the first place, but merely anti-Franco, some complied and helped the Germans more closely with their building projects. After the war, these alleged collaborators were confined in a special camp at Adlington, Lancashire, where they were investigated for pro-German activities in France and the Channel Islands (see the *Evening Post* for 26.11.45).

The Spaniards were housed in camps, although a few seem to have found civilian lodgings, and were not ill-treated as were other classes of workers although, doubtless, they were always hungry. Most Spaniards were returned to France in September, 1943, but at the end of the war there were still 35 in Guernsey, 63 in Jersey and three in Alderney. Nearly all were despatched to England in August, 1945, but a few who had married local girls were allowed to remain.

d) *Local labour*: As already described, the German firm of Theodore Elsche began recruiting local labour in August, 1941, and with the arrival of the *OT* in force towards the end of the same year, the 'Situations Vacant' advertisements placed by German contractors became an almost nightly feature in the *Evening Post*. Again, high rates of pay and extra rations were the bait. By October, 1943, it was estimated that some 550 local people in Jersey alone were employed by the *OT*; among these, however, must be counted a fair number of Irishmen, citizens of the Republic of Ireland, who were perfectly entitled to work for the Germans as they were neutrals. Nevertheless, insofar as local labour was concerned, the Germans lumped everyone together as 'English'.

There was another source of local labour, albeit an involuntary one. This consisted of young men who had made nuisances of themselves to the Germans having been, for example, caught out after curfew. Several escapades of this nature would result in them being offered the choice of working for the *Festpistab* or being sent to

Germany. Thus they often finished up working in the tunnels, although 'working' is hardly the correct word for they were more of a hindrance than a help. They carried out minor acts of sabotage whenever they could and, at the end of the day, anything in the way of tools or other useful items left lying around stuck to their fingers and went home with them!

outright that, like many others, he did it for purely financial reasons, not being able to manage on the weekly wage of £2-10s-0d (£2.50), which was all the States of Jersey, by German decree, was permitted to pay its own workforce. The problem of local people working for the Germans is covered in fine detail in *The German Occupation of Jersey Day by Day*, the personal diary of Deputy Edward

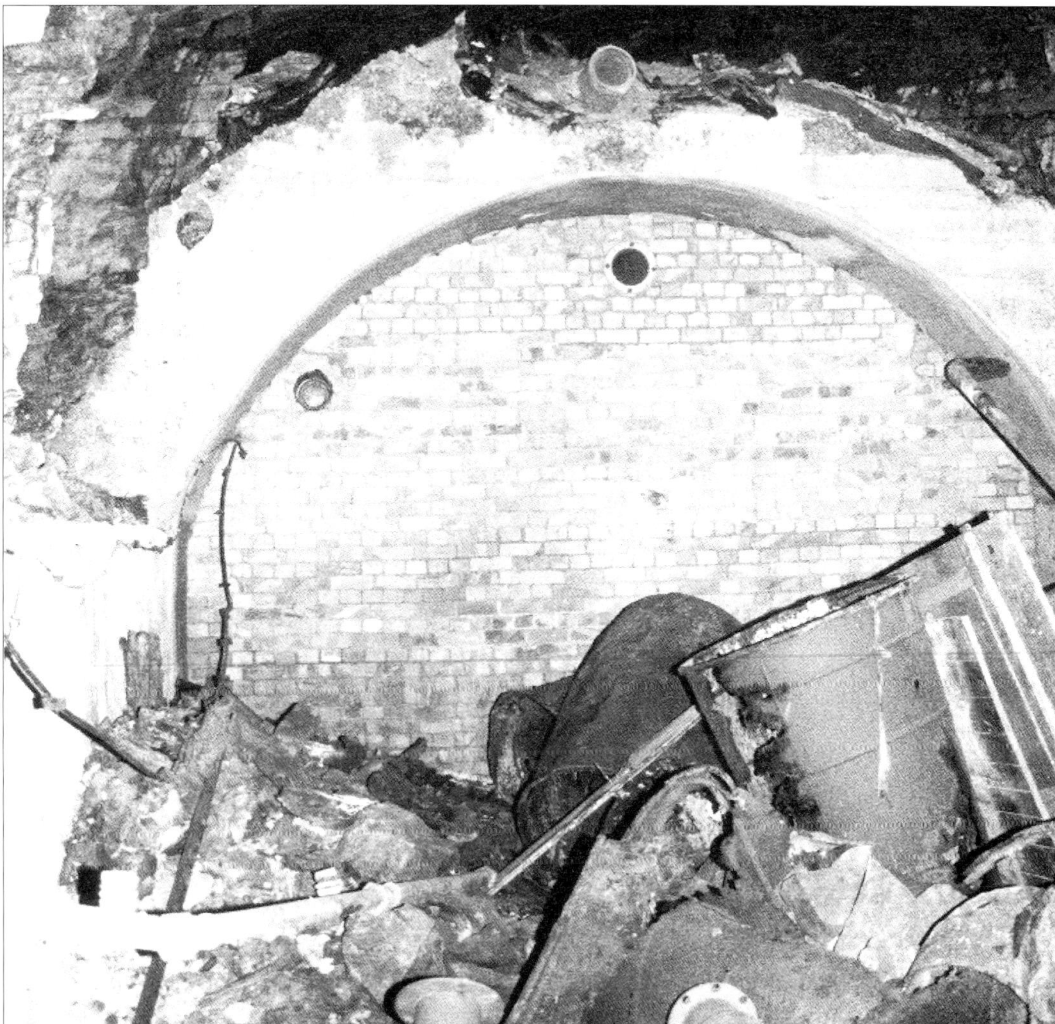

Fig. 8 - Part of the Jersey War Tunnels that the public does not see. These brick walls were erected by Italians in 1944 to convert incomplete galleries into wards.

However, it has to be said that there was a fair number of purely local people who worked for the *OT* quite voluntarily. One who was interviewed while gathering material for this book admitted

Le Quesne, President of the States Department of Labour, 1940-1945 (see pages 10 *et seq*.)

e) *Slave workers*: Although the workers in this category have always been referred to as 'Russians', the greater number consisted of Ukrainians, plus a few Poles and other East Europeans. They were all rounded up by the Germans in their homelands under a compulsory work recruitment scheme - which in practice often meant being rounded up in the street when even schoolboys were likely to be swept into the net. They were shipped to the West for heavy labour, arriving in Alderney and Jersey in August, 1942. Curiously, few seem to have found their way to Guernsey.

Due to the appalling conditions in which they lived and worked, a legend has grown up around this category of workers which leads many people to believe that the Russians/Ukrainians (hereinafter all referred to as 'Russians') provided all the labour for the fortification building programme, particularly in Jersey. In fact, numbering some 1,200 in all, they comprised about one fifth of the total workforce in the Island.

So strongly was this legend put forward in the then German Military Underground Hospital, that the late *Señor* Pascal Pomar, a former Spanish forced labourer and founder member of the Association for Deportees, Resistants and Political Prisoners, was moved to write to the Hospital's proprietors and point out that long before the Russians arrived, much work had already been carried out by the Spaniards and other classes of workers mentioned above.

In pursuance of Nazi party policy the Russian slave workers were considered to be *Untermenschen* (inferior people) and were treated as such. Badly fed and clothed, they often dropped dead at work through sheer exhaustion, being treated as beasts of burden by their overseers who would knock them about with whatever came to hand if they did not move themselves quickly enough.

The Russians were housed in hutted camps and most were returned to France in October, 1943, where they worked on launching sites for flying bombs; when the Allies landed in Normandy in June, 1944, many of these workers made off into the woods and eventually gave themselves up to American troops. They were closely interrogated and so able to reassure British Intelligence that the tunnels in which they had worked in the Channel Islands were purely for storage purposes and were not underground installations for secret weapons. (NA document WO 199/2090A 55851).

Although the number of deaths among the Russian workers will always be open to dispute, the official German total for burials was:- Alderney 369; Jersey 73; Guernsey 1. The last quoted figure lends support to the statement that few Russians worked in that island.

f) *Italians*: When Italy capitulated in September, 1943, some 41,057 Italian troops were trapped by the Germans in that part of south-eastern France which they had been occupying. A small number was still fired with sufficient Fascist zeal to continue to fight alongside the Germans; another 10,225 wanted nothing more to do with war and were shipped off to Germany as prisoners-of-war where they worked in factories, mines, etc.; while the greatest number took the middle course and agreed to continue to work for the Germans as *Hilfswilligen* (auxiliaries). This last named category was permitted to continue to wear their uniforms and to retain their bayonets, but not to carry other arms (A.Wilt, *The Atlantic Wall*, pp. 74-77).

Several hundred of these *Hilfswilligen* arrived in Jersey on 23rd and 27th October 1943 (Sinel's *Diary* refers), and were allocated to German units in small numbers to carry out fatigues, or to act as drivers of horse drawn transport. However, at the end of the same year a decision was taken to convert the tunnel *Ho 8* from an artillery complex into a *Truppenverbandsplatz* (Casualty Receiving Station) and any Italian who followed the trade of bricklayer or plasterer in civilian life was rounded up to work in the tunnel, hastily converting unfinished galleries into hospital wards, an operating theatre, staff quarters, etc.

All the above classes of workers were employed by the *OT* in the construction of the Channel Islands' tunnels. A very few, such as *Ho 1* in La Route de l'Aleval, St. Peter, were constructed by purely voluntary labour, but in the majority of cases workers of all types were employed.

4. Construction

The pedant might well argue that the correct word for the creation of a tunnel should be 'excavation' rather than 'construction'; however, in view of the vast amount of building work that went on inside and around the Channel Islands' tunnels, it has been decided that the latter word is better suited.

The information in this chapter has been gleaned largely from Ralph Ellington's *The German Underground Hospital* which, to date, has been the only published work to give a full and reasonably accurate description of the construction of the German tunnels. While there were, of course, certain detail differences in the methods used by the various contractors, the following may be taken as a general rule:-

Excavation

When a suitable site had been settled upon for the location of a tunnel, almost the first task to be undertaken was the erection of sheds to house the allied trades such as carpenters and blacksmiths. The two trades were much in demand, the former to shape and erect the wooden shuttering in preparation for the pouring of the concrete, and the latter to maintain a constant supply of sharpened steel bits for the pneumatic drills. These drill bits, which varied in length from between one to nine feet, became blunted very quickly and had to be replaced or re sharpened. Compressors were located outside the tunnel entrances and were kept running 24 hours a day and, frequently, seven days a week. When one broke down, or required servicing, a spare compressor was always waiting to take over.

The method of drilling was as follows:- a series of about eight holes, three metres deep (just under ten feet) was drilled in a semi-circle roughly conforming to the intended size of the tunnel; then in the centre three more holes were drilled. When this had been completed, charges were inserted into the central holes and ignited; the process was then repeated with the outer holes, and thus the basic outline of the tunnel was created.

Blasting usually took place every 12 hours, some two hours before the end of each shift, thus leaving time for the dust and fumes to clear. A 60cm gauge railway was laid as close as possible to the rubble, which was loaded into side-tipping railway wagons by slave workers; these were in such poor shape that it took two of them to operate one shovel. The method used was to tie a rope around the head of the shovel. One man would push the shovel into the rubble and the other haul on the rope; both would then lift the shovel to tip the rubble into the wagon. Once the wagons were loaded, they were pushed to the tunnel entrance where they were made up into trains drawn by small diesel locomotives.

These trains proceeded to the chosen dumping site, which usually proved to be the bed of the valley in which the tunnel was being excavated. By this method, the floors of many Island valleys were raised by as much as 12 feet (7 metres), rendering them unsuitable for further cultivation; this to the benefit, it may be added, of post-war housing!

Once the rubble was cleared, the tunnel floor was levelled and temporary roof supports were erected until such time as work was put in hand to remove superfluous rock, and the final size of the tunnel created prior to concreting. This was achieved by the use of probing rods or pneumatic hammers, with small explosive charges to remove the more stubborn rock. This was the most dangerous part of the operation when most accidents occurred.

Over the years many writers have stated that Jersey's German tunnels were "... hewn out of good solid Jersey granite". Nothing could be further from the truth! In fact, with the exception of the tunnels at La Folie (*Ho 19*) and in Grands Vaux (*Ho 4, 10* and *12*), all the Jersey tunnels were cut into the Brioverian shales which form most of the centre of the Island. This is a particularly nasty rock formation, so unstable that it can often be picked away with bare fingers. The effect of explosives on this type of rock can be better imagined than described.

Fig. 9 - Already showing signs of decay only seven years after the war, these mouldering pit-props in *Ho 2* show how the roof was temporarily supported during construction. *Jersey Evening Post*

Concreting & Plastering

Once the tunnel bore had been created to the satisfaction of the *OT* site engineer, concreting and plastering proceeded apace. The first thing to be dealt with was the floor; when concreted it was usual to leave in situ the 60cm gauge railway lines that had been employed to remove the rubble; these then formed the basis of the eventual internal transport system.

On each side of the tunnel floor a nine inch (23cm) footing was provided to form a base for the wooden shuttering. A series of wooden planks was laid on top of each other, horizontally; shored up and blocked off at each end, a box frame was thus created and formed the vertical shuttering for the tunnel wall into which the wet concrete was poured. This was delivered to the work site by hand barrow, carried by two men, from either the tunnel entrance or from the rear of the tunnel into which it had been poured by way of a chute down the embryo escape shaft. The hand barrow was passed up to two other workers who stood on a low scaffolding and the contents were tipped into the box frame.

Once the concrete had hardened, the shuttering was removed and work went ahead on the more difficult roof section. Numbers of curved wooden frames were prepared in advance and these were laid across, and supported by, the newly built vertical walls; planks were then fixed lengthways across these formers, creating a curved box section for the tunnel roof. Liquid concrete was delivered, as before, by hand barrow and this was pushed into the box section by means of long handled tampers.

When the roof formers were removed work began on plastering, although this refinement was more common in those tunnels that were intended for accommodation, rather than storage, purposes. According to Ellington, plastering in *Ho 8* was carried out by local labour who worked on a system of five 10 hour shifts, earning £8.00 per week. However, this was not to the satisfaction of these workers; they complained to the Germans and, after some bargaining, a new piece work rate was thrashed out. Under this new system a crew, consisting of five plasterers and three labourers, had to plaster 35 square yards per shift, including the moving of their own scaffolding as the work progressed. It was due to this piece work system that their take home pay rose to the unheard of sum (for those days) of £12.00 per week!

Fig. 10 - Sketch showing shuttering in position for pouring the concrete to line the vertical walls.

Once the plastering had been completed, the installation of internal fittings was carried out. This included the erection of dividing walls to form storerooms and the installation of plumbing, electrical fittings, etc. However, apart from the electrical fittings, this type of work was, once again, more commonly found in the accommodation tunnels.

Working Conditions

A number of publications have laid great stress on "... the terrible working conditions endured by the slave workers in the tunnels."

Let us, however, be strictly objective about this. In the first place, as already described, not all the workers in the tunnels were slave workers and, in any case, the German *OT* overseers (usually three to a gang of 12 to 15 labourers) worked alongside their charges and shared the dangers; secondly, tunnelling is an inherently arduous and dangerous task whenever and wherever it takes place - the Channel Tunnel, despite all modern technology and safety practices, claimed at least 12 lives during the course of its construction.

With this in mind, it would be reasonable to say that the working conditions inside the Channel Islands' tunnels were no worse than those endured by the navvies who excavated scores of tunnels during the railway mania which gripped Britain during the mid-19th Century. In those days, when safety practices were virtually non-existent, and urged on to even greater efforts by the site engineer who, in turn, had the shareholders breathing down his neck, the railway navvies suffered roof-falls, the premature detonation of unstable gun-powder, flash floods when underground springs were broached, and the tramplings of terrified horses. The drilling of shot holes was accomplished by two men wielding sledgehammers striking a long cold chisel held by tongs in the hands of a third - and all this by the dim illumination of just candles and paraffin flares. The accident rate was absolutely appalling and maiming and sudden death were all a part of daily life.

With pneumatic drills, dynamite, electric light, ventilation and ambulances to remove any injured to the *OT* hospital (such a thing did happen, contrary to popular belief), the 19th Century railway navvies would have considered the tunnellers of the *OT* to be extremely fortunate indeed with their working conditions!

Fig. 11 - Curved roof formers in position for lining the roof section (both sketches were re-drawn by Dave Williams from the originals in *The German Underground Hospital*).

What was at fault with much of the foreign workforce of the *OT* was the shocking treatment they endured, lack of food, poor living conditions and the political and military circumstances that had caused them to be snatched from familiar surroundings and separated from their families, not knowing when, if ever, they would see them again.

The Fortification Programme Slows Down

Hitler's obsession with the Channel Islands was so intense in October, 1941, that he ordered that nothing whatsoever was to interfere with the fortification programme, not even the construction of the main Atlantic Wall on which work started in December of the same year.

Thus, construction of the Channel Islands' tunnels continued unabated once the *OT* was established in the Islands at the end of 1941. However, suddenly, in October, 1943, work came to a virtual standstill. Two factors accounted for this – first, the famous Dam Busters raid of May, 1943, caused such havoc to the German war effort that Dr. Albert Speer who, by this time, had succeeded Dr. Todt as head of the *OT* (the latter having been killed in a still unsatisfactorily explained air crash in Russia in February, 1942), ordered that no less than 7,000 workers be transferred from the Atlantic Wall to Germany to assist in damage repair work.

Secondly, the withdrawal of Italy from the war in September, 1943, meant that new fortifications were required on the Franco-Italian border in order to forestall a possible Allied advance through Italy. The *OT* workforce weathered the first drain on resources (although the Rock Drilling and Mining Companies of the Army Construction Battalions were despatched to other theatres of operations in July, 1943), but the Italian Armistice put the writing on the wall.

By this time Hitler had far more important things to occupy his attention than the Channel Islands, and somebody in the hierarchy of the Fortress Engineers must have decided that the Islands' fortification programme was sufficiently advanced for the workforce to be run down. Accordingly, most of the Russian/Ukrainian (apart from those who had escaped and were in hiding) and North African workers, as well as most of the Spaniards, were transferred to other spheres of operations. Some went to the Pas de Calais area, as well as to the Cotentin peninsula, to build flying bomb and rocket launching sites, while others were rushed to south-eastern France to build yet more fortifications in that region.

The critical months were September and October, 1943 (see Sinel's *Occupation Diary*, entries for 30.9.43 and 31.10.43), when most of the Fortress Engineer staff, the Construction Battalions, the civilian contracting firms, and about four fifths of the foreign workforce were withdrawn.

All that remained was *Abschnittgruppe II* of *Festpistab 19* to control operations in all the Islands; three or four contracting firms in each Island; and about 1,000 workers each in Guernsey and Jersey and a few hundred in Alderney. The *Festpistab* Monthly Building Progress Reports (which, in fact, record no progress at all during this period) complained at length that it was proving impossible to meet designated targets due to the run down of the workforce.

All this is borne out by the childhood memories of Mrs. Margaret Long who lived with her parents at 'Lowlands', Beaumont Valley, and adjacent to the tunnels *Ho 13* and *Ho 15*. She well remembers the daily bustle and activity that went on all day long, practically on the front doorstep; the family home and horticultural business were under threat from the heap of spoil which had been excavated from the tunnels and was being tipped onto the floor of the once lovely valley, advancing inexorably towards the house. Indeed, her father had been warned that, when ordered, they would have to evacuate the property. Suddenly, in October, 1943, the contracting firm began to dismantle all the elaborate equipment that had been erected nearby; in a short space of time it was all loaded onto lorries and taken off to the Harbour, together with the workers, and shipped to France. Nobody came to work anymore – the *OT* had gone and the house, as well as what was left of the valley, was spared.

Thereafter, work continued in some tunnels at a greatly reduced rate. It is known that, in Jersey, Elsche's voluntary workforce carried on with

Ho 15, and did some hasty repair work to *Ho 19* at La Folie; work commenced on the conversion of the proposed artillery barracks/workshops *Ho 8* into a Casualty Receiving Station (*Hauptverbandsplatz*), and this is where the Italians were first employed; and in *Ho 1* and *Ho 2*, La Route de l'Aleval, where some work was done using a somewhat disgruntled workforce in the shape of a group of local tradesmen who had been rounded up in April, 1943 (voluntarily or otherwise), and sent to Alderney to carry out work of a non-military nature, i.e. repairing houses, etc. Returned to Jersey in October of the same year, they thought that they would be able to resume their normal employment but fate and the German authorities decreed otherwise and they found themselves working in the aforementioned tunnels whether they liked it or not! (see letters in the *Evening Post*, issues dated 3, 5, & 7.12.45, and especially a report of an election meeting in the issue dated 10.12.45).

With the advent of D-Day on 6th June 1944, and the subsequent advance of the Americans towards St. Malo in July, the bulk of the remaining *OT* workforce was removed from the Channel Islands before they were cut off. This move occurred towards the end of the same month and it must be assumed that little or no work was done in the tunnels thereafter, especially in view of the fact that two months earlier Leslie Sinel recorded in his *Diary* that "... the Germans have been moving foodstuffs etc., from their usual stores and placing them in some of the tunnels which they have constructed, more especially in St. Peter's Valley and Grands Vaux." (see entry for 22.5.44). Again, on 11.6.44, he records that "... underground hospitals [*sic*] are also fully equipped and ready for use." The use of the plural is of interest but, all the same, not more than one subterranean hospital has ever been recorded in Jersey.

On 20th June 1944, Sinel mentions that "... the Germans are transferring large quantities of ammunition from Fort Regent to their tunnel in Grands Vaux." Therefore, by this date, it can be safely assumed that all work in these tunnels had ceased.

Fig. 12 - The culvert which was intended to cover the stream running down Beaumont Valley. Had tunnelling not ceased in the autumn of 1943, the entire valley floor would have vanished beneath 12 feet of rubble.

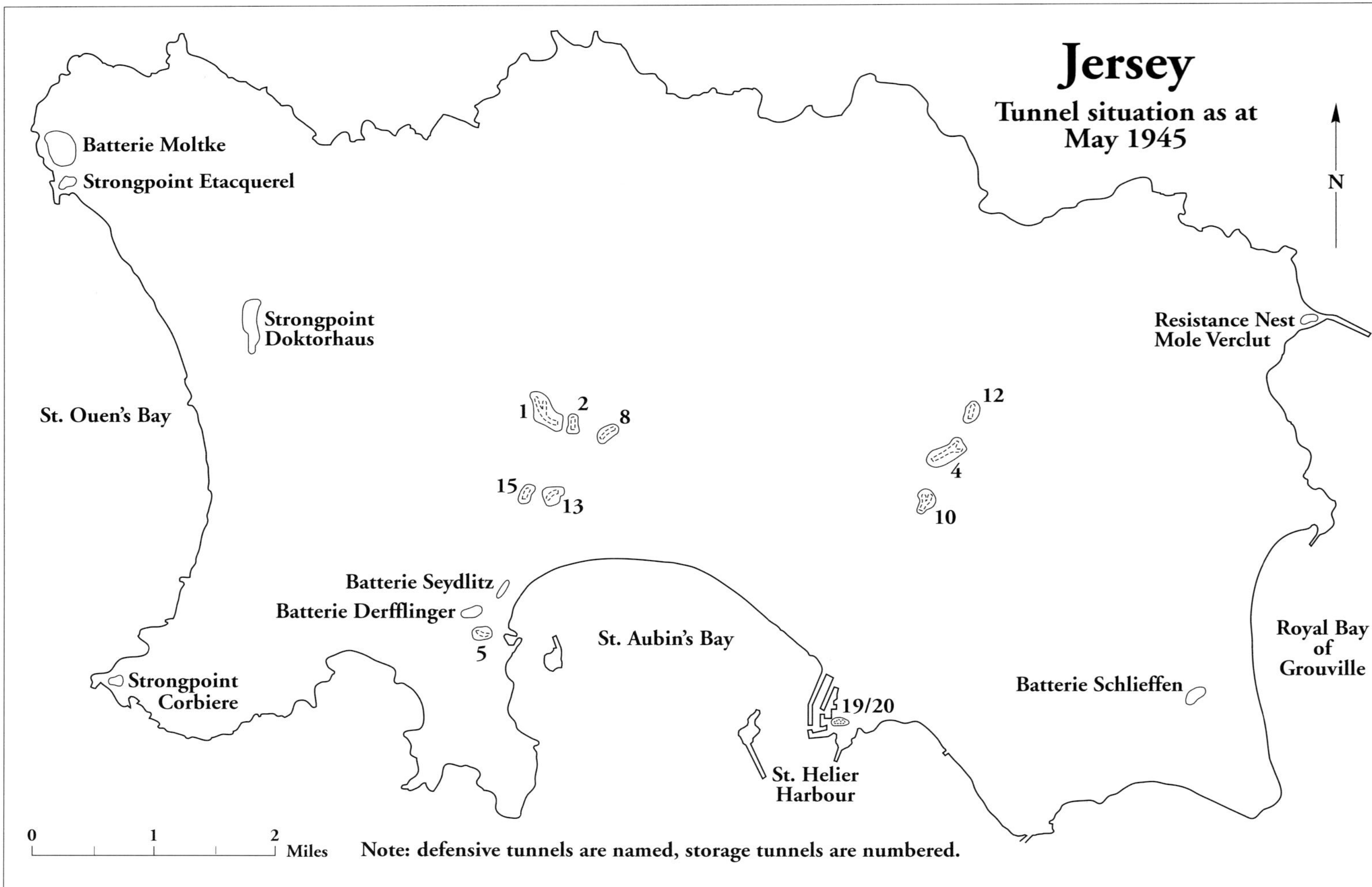

Fig. 13 - Map of Jersey showing the location of all tunnels and 'cut-and-cover' subterranean passages that existed in 1945.

5. The Tunnels

In the absence of any other genuine and original documentary evidence, the information for the total number of tunnels planned for Jersey, as well as their intended purpose, must be taken from the monthly Fortress Engineers Building Progress Reports and the two maps that accompany them. The latter are dated May, 1942, and July, 1943. There may well have been other maps produced at one time or another but, if they were, none appears to have survived.

As is often the case, however, these monthly reports, as well as the maps, pose as many questions as they answer. Each report gives the total square meterage of floor space planned (but not, rather curiously, the cubic capacity); the amount under construction; and the amount completed and ready for use.

The total square meterage of tunnel floor space planned for Jersey was 18,000, yet by June, 1943, the actual amount under construction was given as 20,925m^2. This increase was due to a standardisation of the profile of cross galleries in the tunnels which involved widening the diameter. By May, 1944, the total had increased still further to 23,495m^2, with 2,794m^2 actually completed and ready for use. Although this amounted to 8,829m^2 more than was originally planned, the Reports still showed a total of 18,000m^2.

A further complication arises from the fact that the total number of tunnels shown on the maps varied and, indeed, there are gaps in the numbering sequence. Why, if the planned total was known from the outset, were they not all shown in May, 1942? The map for this particular month gives no indication whatsoever of the intention to excavate *Ho 19*, the Harbour Electricity Generating Station, at La Folie, St. Helier. Yet in his *Diary* Leslie Sinel notes on 31st July that "… among the many blasting operations which are taking place is a huge tunnel being made at the bottom of Mount Bingham."

Unless some new and genuine documentary evidence is forthcoming, it is doubtful if we will ever know the answer.

What we do know, however, is that the map for May, 1942, shows a total of 14 tunnels numbered from *Ho 1* to *Ho 14*. The July, 1943, map adds *Ho 15* and *Ho 19*, as well as two defensive tunnels, namely *Ho Mole Verclut* at St. Martin on the east coast (Verclut Point is the correct name for the area more commonly known as St. Catherine's Breakwater), and *Ho Etacquerel*, St. Ouen, on the west coast. Tunnels *Ho 16*, *17* and *18* are omitted.

A possible solution was a listing of the tunnels once displayed in the late Joe Mière's collection inside *Ho 8*, the then German Military Underground Hospital. Over a period of 17 years Joe built up an impressive collection of photographs and documents given to him by visitors to the tunnels as well as from other sources. As a result, one corner of the exhibition was devoted to tunnels, and on display were the British Army plans of 1962 as well as photographs, both contemporary (c.1945) and modern. Also shown was a listing of the Jersey tunnels which not only agreed with the *Festpistab* maps, but went on to fill in the gaps in the list and added tunnels numbered as high as *Ho 25*. Upon enquiry, Joe stated that this additional information was supplied by a *Herr* Karl Meyer, one of the few former *OT* officials who have returned to Jersey on holiday since the war.

It may well be that *Herr* Meyer once had access to other *Festpistab* maps and intentions which did not survive the war to be preserved in official archives. These could have been part of the Second Construction Programme. It is necessary to explain that when Hitler ordered the permanent fortification of the Channel Islands, two Construction Programmes were put into operation.

The First Programme was due to be completed in 14 months, by April, 1943, and was intended to provide for the defence of the Islands while the war was in progress; it was this Programme that the Fortress Engineer Progress Reports cover. (In the event, even this project was never completed due, mainly, to a shortage of cement caused by the Royal Air Force bombing the railways in France).

The Second Construction Programme, for which no less than eight years were allocated, was intended to secure the Channel Islands for Germany once she had won the war and included even more massive defence works than those of the incomplete First Programme that survive today. It could well be that the higher numbered tunnels mentioned by the former *OT* official were to be included in this Second Construction Programme.

However, this is conjecture, and in the following listing we will refer to these extra tunnels (*Ho 16 -18* and *Ho 20 - 25*) as being on the 'Meyer List' and therefore of uncertain origin. For while the numbers and intended purposes of some of them have a genuine ring about them, the remainder (and particularly the higher numbered examples) are distinctly suspect and must remain so until their provenance is authenticated by a genuine primary source.

La Route de l'Aleval, St. Peter / St. Lawrence

Ho 1 **: Munition Store I** - West side of valley, in the Parish of St. Peter.

Fig. 14 - The lower (southern) entrance of *Ho 1*. Note the granite keystone bearing the crossed hammer emblem of the *RAD* (*Reichsarbeitsdienst*).

This tunnel may be regarded as having been constructed to a basic plan used wherever space allowed; the semi-circular layout of the primary galleries, together with the multiple entrances, permitted the unhindered circulation of vehicular traffic and are typical.

Ho 1 was never completed but construction was sufficiently advanced to permit the storage of ammunition from May, 1944, onwards. This was all contained in the lined chambers which lie at right-angles to the primary gallery, being immediately accessible from the unloading platform which incorporates a 60cm gauge railway track. Beneath the platform run the ducts of a very comprehensive drainage system.

A perusal of the plan of *Ho 1* will reveal the 'herring bone' layout of the uncompleted storage chambers which lie to the rear of the complex; these are so arranged that if an accidental explosion occurred, the resulting blast would travel around the tunnel by the easiest route,

Fig. 16 - The *RAD* emblem in close-up. *Tony Pike*

so causing as little damage as possible. Had the tunnel been completed, the main north and south headings would have joined in a large semi-circle identical to the layout of *Ho 4* in Grands Vaux.

Fig. 15 - The central pedestrian entrance of *Ho 1* with the crossed pick and shovel emblem of the *RAD*. *Tony Pike*

As mentioned in Chapter 3, the early work on this tunnel was carried out by the *Reichsarbeitsdienst* but was subsequently taken over by the firm of Theodore Elsche, using mainly local labour. One local informant who worked in *Ho 1* recalls a Dutch foreman who wore civilian clothes with an *Org. Todt* armband, and that due to Elsche being a careful employer, accidents were few and far between. The only one that he could recall involved two Belgians who were standing on a ladder drilling upwards to create the escape shaft; not surprisingly, the ladder gave up the unequal struggle and collapsed.

However, another accident did occur on 6th February 1942, when the *Evening Post* reported that a telephone call had been received from the

Victoria Hotel, St. Peter's Valley, asking for an ambulance to be despatched to a "spot near there" where a local man had suffered serious injury when a detonator had exploded prematurely, blowing off his left thumb and part of his forefinger. The "spot near there" was obviously *Ho 1.*

blockwork. According to Major F. Sargent, RAOC, the officer responsible for clearing up the Island in 1945/46, similar weapons were placed in uncompleted galleries and the ends blown in (see Appendix I). The *Evening Post* of the day (see issue for 23.2.46) thought the whole scheme

Fig. 17 - Major Sargent, RAOC, and an *Evening Post* reporter near the northern entrance of *Ho 1* in February, 1946. The stripes on the wall are to indicate to a driver that he is approaching a corner. *Jersey Evening Post*

Ammunition was moved into *Ho 1* in May, 1944, and by the end of the war some 6,000 tons were housed in the complex; had it been finished, the British Army estimated that the tunnel could have held no less than 20,000 tons (see 'The Army's Grand Job' in the *Evening Post* for 23.2.46).

By the end of 1945, once the ammunition had been removed for disposal, the British Army saw *Ho 1* as a suitable place for disposing of some items of former German equipment that they did not have time to dump at sea. Consequently, numbers of self-propelled anti-tank guns, mounted on Renault tank chassis, were pushed into the furthest recesses of the tunnel and many *2cm Flak 38* anti-aircraft guns were placed in the completed chambers and sealed in with concrete

to be a good idea and said that "... The bits that do not rust away will provide interesting material for a future archaeologist." However, any future archaeologists will be doomed to disappointment; scrap metal has its price and in 1953 a major scrap drive was initiated when Messrs. Upham's from Guernsey arrived in the Island to remove as much German metalwork as they could lay their hands on.

Consequently, the anti-aircraft guns in the completed chambers were quickly extracted, (those in the blown-in galleries had perforce to remain *in situ*), while the self-propelled anti-tank guns were hauled out, with seized tracks squealing in protest and striking sparks from the concrete floor, all to be cut up into handy parcels of scrap for removal to blast furnaces in England.

Fig. 18 - Major Sargent, with the *Evening Post* reporter in the main primary gallery. *Jersey Evening Post*

Fig. 19 - Time stands still; Ian Chatterley and Matthew Costard in the same spot 66 years later.
Tony Pike

Fig. 20 - The main primary gallery taken from the southern entrance, facing north-east. Note the unloading platform on the left. ***Tony Pike***

Fig. 21 - The central pedestrian tunnel. ***Tony Pike***

Thereafter, *Ho 1* had a variety of uses, providing winter storage space for laid up hire cars or coaches, while some galleries were used by a miniature rifle club. Subsequently, and for many years, *Ho 1* was used for the growing of mushrooms under the auspices of Jersey Mushroom Growers Ltd., and consequently became known as 'The Mushroom Tunnel'. A victim of rising costs, the mushroom farm ceased operating in 2006.

Fig. 22 - The cultivation of mushrooms was pursued in the unlined northern section of the tunnel, with pit-props put in position to support the roof.

The mushroom cultivation took place mainly in the completed chambers that lie alongside the main primary gallery; the passageway leading to the main pedestrian entrance, as well as the short passage containing the eastern escape shaft, was given over to offices, staff accommodation, toilets, etc.

While the incomplete lower, or southern section, of the complex was abandoned and left to its own devices, the partially completed northern section was also used for mushroom growing. Here, Jersey Mushroom Growers carried out some remedial work by partially concreting the floors and installing pit-props, netting and steel girders (in some cases lengths of old German railway lines) to support the roof.

Fig. 23 - Here, the roof is supported by old German railway lines.

It is in the extremities of this northern section that we encounter the two galleries whose ends were blown in by Major Sargent to entomb German equipment. However, whilst it is practically certain that this equipment remains *in situ* (and no doubt in such a degraded state as to be practically worthless), the question that naturally arises is – how extensive is the tunnel complex beyond the rockfalls? As the answer requires a somewhat lengthy explanation, this is examined in more detail in Appendix I, 'The Enigma of *Ho 1*'.

Ho 2 : Ration Store I - East side of the valley, in the Parish of St. Lawrence.

Like *Ho 1*, this tunnel was constructed with multiple entrances and semi-circular primary galleries and, indeed, could be said to be a mirror image of its neighbour just across the valley. (In passing, it should be mentioned that the St. Peter/St. Lawrence parish boundary runs along the centre of the valley which accounts for the fact that the two tunnels are situated in different parishes). However, as the complex was intended as a ration, rather than an ammunition, store it lacks the 'herring bone' layout of storage chambers. Tunnelling began in 1942, the work being carried out by the German contracting firm of J. Witt of Saarbrücken, using French North African forced labourers and Russian slave labourers. Consequently, the workers were badly treated and accidents were frequent. By mid-1944 construction was far from complete.

The primary galleries were still unlined and remain so today; yet the main galleries in the centre of the complex are completed to a very high standard indeed. Obviously, liquid concrete must have been poured down the escape shaft rather than carried in from the entrances. The rearmost galleries have their walls lined but the roof sections are still rough and unshaped.

With the removal of the main *OT* workforce in October, 1943, local workers (both voluntary and involuntary) who had recently returned from Alderney, were put to work inside *Ho 2* under the aegis of Theodore Elsche, but progress was slow and, eventually, all attempts to finish the work were abandoned in late 1944. However, one curious story concerning *Ho 2* was told by a local man working for Elsche; he alleges that during a break on one night shift inside *Ho 1*, he and a friend – out of curiosity – wandered into *Ho 2* to see what was going on; to their surprise, they claim, they came upon a short row of wooden cubicles inside the one completed gallery wherein sat German Army wireless operators manning their sets. At daybreak, they looked up at the hillside over the tunnel entrance and noticed, for the first time, the protruding radio antennae.

Fig. 24 - At the middle of the *Ho 2* complex the tunnel lining has been completed and finished to a very high standard. The letters 'T.E.' on the railway wagon, which has now been removed for preservation, indicate the firm of Theodore Elsche, which was working in this tunnel in 1944. The main contractor had been the firm of J. Witt of Saarbrücken. ***Colin Isherwood***

Fig. 25 - This view of one of the off-shoots from the main primary gallery, with the 60cm railway lines still in position, clearly shows the stratification of the rock. ***Steve Powell***

Fig. 26 - At the rear of the complex, unusually, the walls have been completed before the shape of the roof has been formed. ***Steve Powell***

There is no hard evidence to support this story but certainly, in the gallery indicated, there survive today traces of brackets which could well have supported wooden cubicle walls.

In 1945/46 the British Army decided, as in the case of *Ho 1*, that the tunnel would be an ideal place to dispose of former German equipment that they had been unable to dump at sea. Consequently, into *Ho 2* went field kitchens, range-finders, drums of carbide, cylinders of acetylene gas, field telephones, thousands of respirators and an equally enormous quantity of the ubiquitous steel helmets – a recipe, as it turned out, for tragedy.

The tunnel entrances were then sealed but not substantially enough, and it was not long before intruders burrowed down into the northern adit. Early intruders were seeking non-ferrous scrap metal which commanded a high price in those days - for example, one regular visitor spent hours inside *Ho 2* removing brass fittings from respirators. After some years, however, the younger generation began to take an interest in former German equipment for its souvenir value and, as word spread that *Ho 2* was full of 'stuff' (in passing, why do collectors and dealers always refer to German equipment as 'stuff'?), the tunnel became a place of pilgrimage, especially at weekends.

The first sign of impending disaster came on the evening of 18th March 1952, when two youths set off to explore *Ho 2* with (so they said later) the intention of obtaining wood to make a toolbox. Fortunately, they had told a friend where they were going so that when they had failed to return home by next morning, the youths' fathers, together with the police, were able to mount a search.

Foolishly, the youths had entered *Ho 2* with only

Fig. 27 - Sealed by the military in 1946, this photograph shows the lower entrance of *Ho 2* after it had been breached as a result of one of the many illicit incursions in the 1950s. *Jersey Evening Post*

Fig. 28 - Our intrepid survey team outside the same entrance in 1991. The steel doors were fitted at the time of the official re-opening of the tunnels in 1972.

one torch between them and without the slightest knowledge of the layout of the tunnel which, at that time, was still crammed with German equipment of all shapes and sizes. Their torch failed when they were in the heart of the complex and they were totally lost; unable to find their way out, they spent the entire night blundering about the tunnel looking for the exit, and were considerably relieved when the rescue party arrived at about 9.00am the following morning. The *Evening Post* of 19th March 1952 took a serious view of the matter and said "... These tunnels are in a very dangerous condition and the authorities should take steps immediately to have them effectively sealed up before other persons are trapped and a tragedy has to be recorded."

The entrance was sealed immediately but, youth being what it is, it was not long before a new hole had been burrowed and things continued as before. The *Evening Post* fired further warning shots in 1960 and drew attention to the fact that "... every Sunday afternoon it is not unusual to see anything up to 20 bicycles lying outside the entrance to the incomplete German tunnel behind the Victoria Hotel in St. Peter's Valley while their owners explore the interior." Once more, the paper exhorted the authorities to seal the tunnel properly, again pointing out that unless something was done a disaster would occur. Time was to prove the *Post* to be correct.

In the event, tragedy eventually struck on the afternoon of Sunday, 27th May 1962, when two 15/16 year-old pupils of Victoria College were overcome by fumes in the tunnel and asphyxiated. After exhaustive investigations it was eventually established that the tragedy was due to a bonfire having been lit in the tunnel a few days previously; with only one small (and illicit) entrance to *Ho 2* being open at the time, no air was able to circulate and all the oxygen in the tunnel had been consumed.

This, however, was unknown at the time and it was thought that leaking cylinders of poisonous gas were responsible. As might be expected, the national press had a field day – 'NAZI CYANIDE GAS KILLS TWO YOUTHS' screamed the headlines, and this was followed by graphic descriptions of how the Germans were intending to exterminate the entire civilian population of the Channel Islands using the gas cylinders found inside *Ho 2*.

A preliminary inquest was held within two days when it was established that (i) the cause of death was due to carbon monoxide poisoning; (ii) there was absolutely no trace whatsoever of cyanide gas anywhere inside the tunnel; and (iii) the gas cylinders, which in any case were empty, had contained nothing more lethal than acetylene gas for welding equipment. Deprived of anything sensational to embellish upon, the reporters of the national press slunk away disappointed but no correction was ever published by them. It was left to the *Evening Post* to print the true facts which can be followed up in all issues from 28th May 1962, onwards. The entire sad story was front page news for a whole week, with the results of the final inquest being published on 25th July 1962.

To help with enquiries into the disaster several military experts were brought in, among them being Mr. A.E. Bradshaw and Dr. J.M. Wright of the Chemical Warfare Staff; Major J. Harrison, RAOC, an ammunition expert, and Wing Commander E.C.R. Bramwell, RAF Medical Services. Their investigations were long and thorough, as were those of the General Hospital and the States Analyst's Department.

During the course of the actual rescue attempts at the scene of the accident, great bravery was shown by members of the States Fire Service, particularly Fireman John Barnes, and several members of the St. John Ambulance Service, who entered the tunnel unprotected in an attempt to effect a rescue. All were overcome by the fumes but, after treatment at the Hospital, they insisted on returning to the scene of the accident to render further assistance. Surprisingly, it would appear

Fig. 29 - Following the case of the missing youths in 1952, an *Evening Post* reporter peers into the hole (upper entrance) through which intruders gained access. *Jersey Evening Post*

Fig. 30 - The same point of entry after it had been cleared by Mr C. Liron in 1986. After the 1962 tragedy the concrete wall was erected to keep out intruders; the small hole at the top right hand corner of the larger aperture shows that it was not very successful!

Fig. 31 - The same adit after clearance work by Mr. Liron.

that no proper breathing apparatus was available in those days for it was left to two police frogmen, Corporal Medder and PC John Faiers, assisted by Mr. Tony Titterington of the British Sub-Aqua Club, all wearing underwater breathing apparatus, to carry out a thorough exploration.

In passing, it may be mentioned that although *Evening Post* photographers took many (and in some cases, dramatic) photographs of the rescue operations, for one reason or another most have vanished without trace!

Eight weeks elapsed between the initial accident and the final verdict of death through misadventure being given by the inquest jury. During this time the tunnel had been re-sealed but, hardly had this been done, when further attempts were being made by collectors and others to regain access. At the inquest a spokesman for the then Public Works Department said that since 1954 they had spent more than £500.00 on continual efforts to keep *Ho 2* sealed, but every

Fig. 32 - Inside the same entrance in 1952 with pit-props still in position.
Jersey Evening Post

Fig. 33 - The rockfall marked at A on the tunnel plan (see Appendix III, page 111) which was caused by the fire in 1962, was approximately two feet high in 1972. Today, it is over twelve feet high and doubtless the roof at this point will collapse altogether one day. It is to be hoped that nobody is inside the tunnel when it does!

time the illicit access hole was blocked up, persons unknown came to the spot under the cover of darkness and removed the wet concrete before it had had time to set.

It was the initial opinion of Brigadier D. W. Reid, the Army expert comissioned in June, 1962 to examine the condition of the Island's German tunnels (see Appendix V) that so long as German relics remained in *Ho 2*, the curious and/or acquisitive would always make efforts to gain entry, and that all such relics should be removed in order to prevent further accidents. The fact that the two unfortunate youths were suffocated was a freak and would not have happened had not the bonfire been lit in the tunnel; far more prevalent, however, was the ever present danger of roof-falls in a tunnel which was largely unlined. This danger was enhanced by the bonfire which had rendered the rock overhead friable, and thus even more unstable, and this has indeed subsequently caused a major rockfall at this point.

By the time he presented his final report in August, 1962, Brigadier Reid had reconsidered his earlier advice and concluded that the removal of artefacts from *Ho 2* would be too hazardous owing to the presence of calcium carbide. An effort to seal the tunnel properly was made by inserting a three feet concrete 'plug' into the hole through which intruders gained access. However, as the Brigadier himself had predicted, this was no obstacle to determined youth and within three months the 'plug' was breached and the entire process began again. Eventually, in 1972, and persuaded by various bodies with pecuniary interests in Occupation relics, the Public Works Committee agreed that *Ho 2* should, once and for all, be cleared out completely. However, having visited the complex on the day that it was opened, and being impressed by what they saw, the members of the Committee decided to extract the worthwhile relics and put them on display at Elizabeth Castle. (See the *Jersey Evening Post* for 1.2.73).

Under the overall supervision of Mr. R. Gibson, the then Art & History Officer of the Public Works Department, and with Mr. Tony Titterington in charge of the working party, work began on the extraction and removal of anything that looked as if it might merit restoration; thus out to Elizabeth Castle went hundreds of steel helmets (these were sand blasted and painted, and sold off to the public at £2.00 each), as well as two 60cm gauge side-tipping railway wagons and several field kitchens. (See the *Jersey Evening Post* for 7.2.75).

Work on recovering the relics proceeded apace for some time until, for some unknown reason, the whole project began to run out of steam; Mr. Gibson resigned from his position for purely personal reasons and returned to England. Thereupon, the upper entrance, which had been the means of illegal access for many years, was solidly sealed, while the lower entrance had a substantial concrete block wall built behind the steel doors which had been fitted in 1972. And that, everyone thought, was the end of the saga of *Ho 2*!

Fig. 34 - A section of the tunnel, crammed full of rusting equipment, as it appeared shortly after the tragedy in 1962. ***Jersey Evening Post***

During the period when these events were taking place the Public Works Committee assumed responsibility for the entire tunnel complex, and could not have checked the boundaries of the land owned by them. This was perhaps fortunate for the owners of the land above, but nonetheless surprising, for in November, 1961, the Royal Court had ruled, once and for all, that anyone who owned land also owned whatever lay beneath it, down to the centre of the Earth (see pages 61-63 for the full details).

Thus, when all the incursions into *Ho 2*, and the accidents resulting therefrom, were taking place, it could well have been that the Public Works Department was not responsible for the tunnel at all; for, apart from a short stretch a few score yards long inside the southern entrance, the major part of the complex belonged (and still does) to the owner of the property known as Walnut Farm which stands above.

This came to light when Walnut Farm was purchased by a Mr. Charles Liron in the early 1980s. Mr. Liron wasted no time in establishing his claim to the tunnel and looked for ways in which *Ho 2* could be commercially developed. The first task was to clear the complex of the detritus which mostly littered the main primary gallery. This was carried out by the late Paul Clothier, proprietor of the then newly opened Island Fortress Occupation Museum in St. Helier, who acquired the rights to clear the tunnel of rusting remains in the hope that amongst them might lie some relic still worth restoring to include in his displays.

In order to accomplish this, it was necessary to open out the small northern entrance which had been the means of access for unauthorised intruders over many years. A stout steel gate was fitted but even this was not vandal proof and was soon wrenched off once word got around that the tunnel was again open (see the *Jersey Evening Post* for 27.6.86).

Fig. 35 - Mr. Liron and digger at the lower entrance prior to serious clearance work in 1988.
Jersey Evening Post

This notwithstanding, the gate was replaced and work on clearing the tunnel pressed ahead. However, it was not long before fears of a second tragedy were raised when a fire broke out due, no doubt, to a lit cigarette end being dropped among the considerable remains of decaying pit-props. The fire smouldered on for some days during which time access was impossible (see the *Jersey Evening Post* for 23.4.87).

Eventually, the tunnel was completely cleared and Mr. Liron first pursued the possibility of converting the complex into underground storage for hire cars laid up during the winter months. When this proved not to be feasible, he applied to convert *Ho 2* into another Occupation museum; not surprisingly, this was turned down by the Island Development Committee on the grounds that this would be an intrusion of a commercial development into the Green Zone (the *Jersey Evening Post* for 22.11.88 refers).

Fig. 36 - A rockfall caused by the natural fault line running the entire length of the tunnel.

Mr. Liron announced that he would appeal against this ruling but was taken ill before he could do so and, regrettably, passed away. Ownership of the tunnel then devolved upon his family, since when no further steps have been taken and today *Ho 2* remains dark, locked and seemingly abandoned. It would be nice to think that some use could be made of this tunnel as it is, without doubt, the most interesting and impressive example of its kind in Jersey.

Fig. 37 - The enormous heap of spoil on the eastern side of the valley as it appeared on ciné film shortly after the Liberation. ***Rolf Bertram***

Fig. 38 - The stone crusher in La Route de l'Aleval in 1945. ***Rolf Bertram***

Before moving on to look at other tunnels, it is necessary to say a few words about the area immediately around *Ho 1* and *Ho 2*. Prior to the autumn of 1941 the valley into whose flanks the tunnels have been bored must have been a haven of beauty and tranquility. Only the narrow lane leading from the Victoria Hotel (rebuilt in the 1980s and now simply known as 'The Victoria') to Panigot ran past the small cottage which still stands outside the entrance of *Ho 1*; and only the sound of contented cows munching grass must have disturbed the peace.

With the arrival of the *RAD* and, later, the *OT*, things rapidly changed. The first spoil resulting from the initial excavations was used to lay a hoggin road, on each side of which were erected the huts to house the allied trades associated with tunnelling; Theodore Elsche even had a shop where his workers could purchase food over and above the normal ration scale. The area soon became a hive of activity, dust and noise.

Rubble resulting from later blasting was loaded into 60cm gauge railway wagons which were pushed to the tunnels' entrances and made up into trains. A small diesel locomotive drew these away and the spoil was tipped onto the eastern side of the valley. The resultant heap grew so large that, at the lower end, where The Victoria car park now stands, it almost towered above the valley side itself. It was enormous and had to be seen to be believed!

After the war the heap was largely reduced by using the stone to infill behind the German anti-tank wall running between Bel Royal and La Haule to create the promenade that we know today; a considerable amount was also consumed in the construction of the various post-war extensions to the main Airport runway at St. Peter (see the *Evening Post* for 19.1.46).

It must be added that the lower end of St. Peter's Valley had a narrow escape. In August, 1943, the German authorities wrote to the Bailiff of Jersey to inform him that as the existing tip was almost full to capacity, they intended to continue to dump spoil from the two tunnels lower down the valley in the direction of Tesson Mill. Had this occurred, the woods and meadows that we know and enjoy today would have been obliterated, but

Fig. 39 - The remains of the stone crusher as it appeared in 1986. It is now heavily overgrown.

by good fortune the rundown of the *OT* commenced two months later and the project was abandoned.

Any interested reader who looks closely in the undergrowth between the two entrances of *Ho 2* will find the heavily overgrown remains of a stone crusher erected at this spot by the *OT*. Curiously, there is no evidence that this was used to crush any of the shale removed from the tunnels; rather, it appears to have reduced stone brought from the quarries at L'Etacq and Ronez, which had been passed through primary crushers at source, and transported to the crusher for further treatment before being used in the aggregate for the concrete lining the tunnels' interiors. An exploratory dig beneath the crusher's remains will reveal stone from both sources. After the war the crusher was re-activated to reduce shale from the tunnels and this was used to repair the Island's roads following five years of neglect (see the *Evening Post* for 19.1.46).

The *OT* extended the hoggin road to the top of the valley to the area known as Le Pissot, and for many years after the war it remained neglected and partially overgrown. Known locally as 'The German Road', it was used mainly by motor cyclists and persons illegally entering *Ho 2*. Eventually, however, the Public Works Department took the road in hand and provided a proper surface. This was in 1966, and for many years the road led virtually nowhere, but today it provides the principal means of access to one of Jersey's tourist attractions, 'The Living Legend'.

Too coy at the time to christen the new road with its correct geographical name of La Route de Pissot (the word 'Pissot' is onomatopoeic and derived from the stream which issues from the rock at the head of the valley), the Public Works Department bestowed the title of La Route de l'Aleval upon the thoroughfare. Had this naming been done today, it is more than likely that the road would have been named La Route des Allemands, which would not only have had historical significance but would have caused future generations to ponder over its origins.

Bellozanne Valley, St. Helier

***Ho 3* : Munition Store II** – West side of the valley, upper end.

Although this tunnel never got beyond the planning stage, from the *Festpistab* map it would appear to have been sited in the vicinity of what was formerly Jersey Coal Distributors' yard.

***Ho 9* : Electricity Generating Station I** – East side of the valley, probably in the vicinity of today's modern waste recycling plant.

The entire German defensive system depended upon the current generated by the Queen's Road power station of the Jersey Electricity Company. This building, however, was located in an extremely open and vulnerable position at Mont à l'Abbé and was an easy target for aerial attack, which accounted for the nearby siting of a heavy, six gun, 8.8cm anti-aircraft battery.

Thus it made sense for the *Festpistab* to create a subterranean power station in a valley as close to Mont à l'Abbé as possible so that it could be linked into the existing mains with a minimum of difficulty. In order to house the necessary machinery, the tunnel would have had to have been of substantial proportions but, even so and in view of its importance to the defence system, it is rather surprising that *Ho 9* never got beyond the planning stage.

Grands Vaux, Trinity

***Ho 4* : Munition Store III** – Situated to the north-west of Paul Mill.

Construction of this tunnel was sufficiently advanced for it to be used for its intended purpose from May, 1944, onwards. *Ho 4* is one of the large complexes and is almost identical in plan to *Ho 1.* A plaque to the rear of the tunnel records that construction was in the hands of the Deutsche Asphalt Company and, while the initial work was doubtless carried out by French and North African forced labourers, Russians were later moved over from the west of the Island to assist. These Russians were housed in a sub-camp inside Huelin's yard at Five Oaks, where the *Schirrhof* (Plant Yard) of the Fortress Engineers was located.

Fig. 40 - The southern entrance to *Ho 4.*
Neil Walker

They were marched on foot to their new quarters and their progress through St. Helier was witnessed by Mr. Harry Aubin's mother and described in his book *The Occupation Bicycle Park* (La Haule Books, 1992, p.80):

I was standing at the top of the path at the side of the house when I noticed a strange shape coming up St. Saviour's Road. This shape took up most of the width of the road and had little recognisable form and to be of a dirty brown dusty colour. In the distance it resembled a very wide silent, mobile cloud or mist moving between the buildings. As it approached, I noticed that it was a large group of closely packed beings, shuffling up the road under guard and in complete silence. They looked emaciated and looked most miserable, dressed in rags and some with sacking on their feet. They were of a range of ages, some being very young, but all were staring straight ahead as if afraid to draw attention to themselves.

With the departure of these Russians in October, 1943, it is said that work was then carried on by a smaller force consisting of voluntary French labour. As usual, the spoil removed was dumped nearby and another once lovely valley ruined. On 4th August 1944, Leslie Sinel's *Diary* records that, in the siege period following the fall of St. Malo during the same month, Dutch seamen from barges laid up in St. Helier Harbour were put to work to create a hoggin road through the upper end of the valley; unlike La Route de l'Aleval in St. Peter, and fortunately for posterity and wild life, this road was not subsequently surfaced and made into a public highway.

On 28th April 1943, Sinel recorded that a premature explosion in a tunnel in Grands Vaux resulted in several casualties being taken to hospital,

Fig. 41 - The tunnel is owned, and used as a store, by Jersey Water. This is the main primary gallery looking towards the sealed northern entrance; note the 60cm railway line running along the unloading platform. ***Neil Walker***

but this did not necessarily occur in *Ho 4* as two other tunnels (*Ho 10* and *Ho 12*) were being excavated simultaneously in Grands Vaux. However, a severe roof-fall occurred in *Ho 4* and this penetrated right through to the surface with consequent interruption to agriculture in a field belonging to Augrès Farm, where a large pit suddenly appeared. This roof-fall is doubtless the reason for the blocked off gallery in the centre of the complex.

Once *Ho 4* had been cleared of ammunition in 1946, the British Army filled the incomplete northern entrance with redundant tank obstacles

Fig. 42 - One of the notable features of *Ho 4* is the meticulously radiused curves of the passages and galleries. This is the access point into the main primary gallery from the southern entrance. ***Neil Walker***

Fig. 43 - In a very similar fashion to *Ho 1*, the main primary gallery of *Ho 4* 'splits' at each end, with the 60cm railway line running in a loop from the loading platform to the rear of the complex. ***Neil Walker***

and masses of barbed wire. The latter was crammed into the tunnel with a bulldozer; packed tight, it remains there to the present day. The entrance was then sealed but following the *Ho 2* tragedy, when the military experts were inspecting all German tunnels, it was noted that youths had also effected illegal entry to *Ho 4* (the *Evening Post* for 1.6.62 refers).

Fig. 44 - One of the side storage galleries. ***Neil Walker***

Since then, *Ho 4* has had a fairly unremarkable life; used as a potato store for many years by Jersey Potato Canners Ltd., most of the tunnel now belongs to Jersey Water, who likewise use it for storage purposes. More interestingly, under the emergency planning provisions for dealing with the anticipated swine flu pandemic in 2010, *Ho 4* would have been pressed into service as a mortuary.

Fig. 45 - At the rear of the complex, the approach loop widens into the main transverse gallery for a straight section roughly equivalent to the length of the side galleries, and then abruptly narrows again. This is not apparent on the plan, which was copied from that drawn up by the British Army in 1962.
Neil Walker

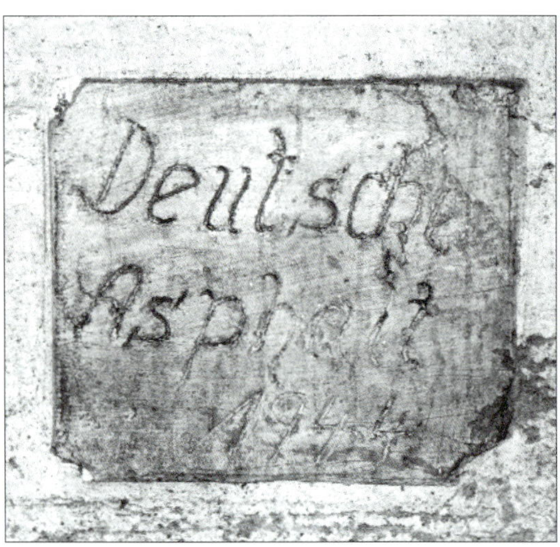

Fig. 46 - The name of the contractor and the date of near completion of the tunnel are to be found on a plaque at the rear of *Ho 4*.

Railway Walk, St. Aubin

***Ho 5* : Fuel Store I** – Located inside the former Jersey Railways & Tramways tunnel at St. Aubin; converted into a munition store in 1944.

The railway tunnel at St. Aubin was opened in December, 1896, by the newly formed JR & T in order to eliminate a series of severe reverse curves which trains of the earlier Jersey Railways Company, proceeding to La Moye, had to negotiate around the foot of the hill through which the tunnel was subsequently bored. When the railway closed in October, 1936, with the track being lifted some six months later, the tunnel was abandoned, its future uncertain. It did see, however, a brief burst of activity on 28th June 1940, when many St. Aubin's residents sought shelter in the tunnel during German air raids.

Fig. 47 - The railway tunnel at St. Aubin as it appeared in 1935; despite the elaborate brickwork at the entrance, the interior was completely unlined. *Jersey Evening Post*

In 1941 the Fortress Engineers lost no time in exploiting the tunnel's potential, setting to work to enlarge the diameter of the original bore whilst leaving the portals unaltered save for the erection of a hefty concrete anti-blast wall hard by the lower entrance; this incorporated a machine-gun loophole which formed the defensive position known as *Widerstandsnest Aubins Ort* (Resistance Nest St. Aubin's Village).

Once the task of enlarging the original bore was complete, the walls were lined with concrete and a main gallery was driven at right-angles into the hillside, this having storage chambers branching off at roughly 45 degrees. Although intended to store fuel, in the event *Ho 5* was used as an ammunition store; this change of use made sense, as the tunnel was situated at a comparatively short distance from the three medium coastal artillery batteries at Noirmont Point, Red Houses and La Moye.

Although it was intended that other tunnels should be supplied by rail, *Ho 5* was the only example to be actually connected to the metre gauge system of the *OT*, on which all trains proceeding to La Moye or Ronez, because of the blast wall obstructing the lower tunnel entrance, had to follow the same sinuous path around the foot of the hill as used by the trains of the erstwhile Jersey Railways. About 100 yards above the upper entrance a trailing junction led back into the tunnel itself where the rails of the metre gauge track may still be seen embedded in the concrete floor. Paralleling this are the tracks of the 60cm gauge internal transport railway.

Fig. 48 - An exact post-war comparison photo is impossible due to the blast wall erected by the Germans, which stands just off the left-hand edge of this picture taken on the occasion of a visit to the tunnel by members of the Société Jersiaise in July, 1946. *Jersey Evening Post*

Fig. 49 - Taken on the same occasion. Note that the interior bore of the original tunnel has been greatly enlarged and is now lined. The metre gauge tracks of the *OT* railway may be seen embedded in the floor. *Jersey Evening Post*

Fig. 50 - The main bore of the German tunnel looking back towards the main gallery. *Tony Pike*

Fig. 51 - A 1945 shot of the interior of *Ho 5* with the main bore of the German tunnel burrowing back into the hillside. Note the ventilation trunking on the right and the tracks of the 60cm gauge internal transport railway in the floor. *F. Sargent*

Fig. 52 - The same view today, with the railway tracks still in place. *Neil Walker*

Fig. 53 - The impressive escape shaft to the rear of the complex.
Tony Pike

The spoil removed during construction was taken down to St. Aubin's Harbour by metre gauge railway and dumped onto the harbour bed, a practice which eventually drew loud cries of protest from the German Navy. The *OT* was then obliged to lay a further length of metre gauge track along The Bulwarks in order to remove the stone from the harbour and dump it onto the shore adjacent to the Royal Channel Islands Yacht Club, converting what was once a reasonably sandy beach into the uncomfortable stony one that exists today. Remnants of the stone on the harbour bed may be seen opposite St. Brelade's Parish Hall.

In an enclave in the hillside further up the Railway Walk a second adit to the tunnel was commenced but not proceeded with, although a few yards survive behind a pile of rubbish; thus *Ho 5* is one of the few tunnels to have been totally lined and completed. For many years now it has served as an equipment store, first under the aegis of the States of Jersey Telephone Department and now for the Transport & Technical Services Department. More recently, as in the case of *Ho 4*, the tunnel would have had a role to play in the anticipated swine flu pandemic, serving as a store for oxygen supplies.

La Petite Route de l'Aleval, St. Peter

Ho 6 **: Personnel Shelter I** – Location uncertain, but should have been in the vicinity of the Fortress Commander's bunker at the *Kernwerk* (Battle HQ).

On page 36 of the 1948 survey of his wartime command entitled *The Channel Islands - Preparations for the Defence against the Invasion, and during the Invasion, until the Surrender*, the former Military Commander of the Channel Islands, *Generalleutnant* Rudolf Graf von Schmettow, wrote, "... on Jersey the

Command Posts were situated in what was called the *Kernwerk* (Inner Fortress Building), in the centre of the island, in a place where the infantry reserves were lying near underground passages."

Additionally, the *Festpistab* Building Progress Report Maps for 1942 and 1943 both show *Ho 6* to be located a short distance from, and to the east of, the Fortress Commander's HQ bunker at the *Kernwerk*. This bunker is the one that for many years was known as 'The Strawberry Farm Bunker', being part of the tourist attraction bearing that name. It has now been absorbed into the larger 'Living Legend' attraction and serves as a storeroom for the complex.

As a result of information given by a local person, an involuntary worker in *Ho 1* in 1943, who stated that he remembered some construction work in progress at the top of "the German road" (now La Route de l'Aleval), it was assumed that this work must have been in connection with the excavation of *Ho 6*. However, it is now known that it was concerned with the creation of well chambers for the proposed water supply for *Ho 1* and *Ho 2* lower down the valley (see Appendix I).

By chance, the recent discovery of paperwork relating to the issue of wood fuel and dated April, 1945, reveals that the reserve troops shared the tunnel *Ho 1* with 6,000 tons of artillery ammunition, whilst the company headquarters were based at the nearby Victoria Hotel.

La Route de Cap Verd, St. Lawrence

***Ho 7*: Reserve Artillery** – Was intended to be situated on the east side of the valley on which stands the housing estate known as Cap Verd.

Although some exploratory work seems to have been carried out, actual construction never got underway. Cap Verd is perhaps better known as the location of the rear entrance of *Ho 8*, the Jersey War Tunnels, which is opposite the intended *Ho 7*.

Meadowbank/Cap Verd, St. Lawrence

***Ho 8*: Artillery Quarters** – Converted into a Casualty Receiving Station (*Hauptverbandsplatz*) in 1944, this tunnel lies in a branch of St. Peter's Valley, leading to the lane Les Charrières de Malorey; the lesser known rear entrance is in Cap Verd.

The *Festpistab* map for 1942 bestows the title of *Artillerieunterkunft* upon this tunnel; the term '*Unterkunft*' may be translated as either 'Quarters' or 'Shelter'. Bearing in mind the fact that Hitler's long-term, eight-year, plan for the permanent fortification of the Channel Islands provided for the installation of one four gun 38cm (15 inch) heavy coastal artillery battery on each of the three larger Islands, it would be reasonable to assume that *Ho 8* was intended to be a large subterranean workshops/store for servicing the guns of the Jersey battery, which was planned to be located at Les Blanches Banques, St. Brelade, as well as providing shelter for the gunners and artificers.

Work on *Ho 8* commenced in September, 1941, employing troops of the Construction Battalions, and the political prisoners from *Lager Ehrenbreitstein* at Fort Regent mentioned in Chapter 3. Construction was handed over to the *OT* at the end of the same year when the German contracting firm of Gremmich began working from the Meadowbank entrance and that of Karl Plötner from Cap Verd. The workforce now consisted of French North Africans, Spaniards and (whether we like it or not) local voluntary labour. The Russians/Ukrainians, who get all the publicity, did not arrive until the latter part of August, 1942. The majority of the foreign workforce was housed in the *OT* camp known as *Lager Schepke* situated on Goose Green Marsh.

Construction followed the usual procedures, with the spoil being dumped into the bed of the valley at Cap Verd, thus making possible the construction of the small, luxury, post-war housing estate at that point. The area surrounding

Fig. 54 - The main (Meadowbank) entrance to *Ho 8*, now known as the 'Jersey War Tunnels'.
Tony Pike

the Meadowbank entrance was vastly different to that seen today, with only a narrow lane as an approach road and a high bank on what is now the car park side. Liquid concrete was brought in via the entrances as well as being poured down the escape shaft by means of a rudimentary chute made of sheets of corrugated iron. It is said that here a Spaniard lost a leg in an accident, and subsequently died, when a sheet became detached and fell the entire length of the shaft.

According to several reports accidents were frequent, and Ellington (*The German Underground Hospital*, p.17) records one incident in which three workers were killed by a rockfall and another, more serious, when 22 workers perished. It is said that some of those killed were left where they were buried beneath the rockfall, it being too dangerous to retrieve the bodies, the affected gallery then being abandoned. Contrary to the story beloved by coach drivers and the early post-war guide books, bodies that were recovered were not tipped into the concrete lining the tunnel, but were removed and buried at the Strangers' Cemetery at Westmount. Neither were all those killed slave workers.

In his book, *Never to be Forgotten*, Joe Mière describes how, during the 17 years that he worked in the tunnel, he often saw the ghost of an *OT* overseer walking the corridors, and he is not alone in this. One night a courting couple, sitting in a car parked at the tunnel entrance, had a nasty fright when the restless spirit not only walked through the iron barred gate, but through the car as well! What confirmed the existence of the ghost in Joe's mind is the fact that all who report seeing the phantom are surprised by the khaki uniform that it wears (not realising that this was the colour of the uniform worn by officials of the *OT*) and not the field-grey of the German Army.

Joe was adamant in his story – those who disbelieve in ghosts (or are afraid to acknowledge their existence) will scoff, but those who do believe will understand.

Fig. 55 - Inside the rear entrance at Cap Verd, with the gas lock doors which were fitted in 1944 when the complex was converted from an artillery quarters into a Casualty Receiving Station. This mirrors the gas door arrangement on the main entrance. *Tony Pike*

Ho 8 is remarkable in that it is the only tunnel in Jersey entirely devoid of curves; practically every corner is a right-angle. It will be noticed that, in common with the other tunnels, all floors slope towards one entrance; this was done to ensure an efficient drainage system, the wooden covered channels of which may be seen set in the floors. Also to be noted are the rails of the 60cm gauge internal railway system which vanish under blank walls, a situation brought about when the complex was converted from artillery workshops into a hospital and the ends of unfinished galleries were bricked up and converted into wards.

During construction some 14,000 metric tons (*tonnes*) of rock were excavated and 4,000 *tonnes* of concrete were poured to line the completed galleries. The total space excavated amounted to 272,000 cubic feet (7,700 cubic metres) and the total floor space created was 2,611 square feet (2,565 square metres). As interesting as the completed sections are, the uncompleted galleries (some of which, although partly visible, are not accessible to the public), are far more impressive, with the intersection of main corridors crowned with a vaulted roof, as in *Ho 2*.

Unlike Guernsey and Alderney, the *Festpistab* map for the First Construction Programme does not show a subterranean *Lazarett* (Hospital) for Jersey; quite possibly this would have been included in the Second Construction Programme – see *Ho 18*. However, when the changing fortunes of war made it obvious that the latter Programme would never see the light of day a decision was taken, probably late in 1943, to convert *Ho 8* into a Casualty Receiving Station. With the bulk of the *OT* workforce by now having been returned to the Continent, it was at this time that the Italian *Hilfswilligen*, as well as tradesmen among the German troops, were brought in (as described in Chapter 3) to complete the plastering and to erect brick walls in order to convert unfinished galleries into wards.

Many people ask why it was necessary to place a hospital underground. Would not an ordinary military hospital clearly marked with Red Crosses have been sufficient? The answer must be "No!" ... in a total war situation, and with the amount of concentrated firepower that would have been necessary to overcome the indisputably formidable German defences of the Channel Islands, everything above ground would have been at risk and the worst fear of troops already wounded is to be caught up in subsequent bombardments. In any case, underground hospitals are not necessarily a German prerogative

Fig. 56 - One of the complex's two Dräger air filtration plants - the only surviving examples of their type left in the world! ***Tony Pike***

Fig. 57 - The central heating plant. *Tony Pike*

– the Rock of Gibraltar, for long a British bastion and outpost of Empire, has not just one, but two underground hospitals.

Furthermore, it is necessary to realise that *Ho 8*, like its Guernsey counterpart, was not intended to be a long stay hospital; this is borne out by some recently discovered wartime maps which detail German medical facilities and First Aid Posts. These make it clear that the correct designation of the so-called hospital was, in fact, *Hauptverbandsplatz*, or Main Casualty Receiving Station. It may thus be deduced that during the height of a battle any casualties would have been conveyed to the tunnel where they would have had their wounds attended to and then put to bed. Once the attacker had been hurled back into the sea, the wounded troops would have been moved to more normal hospital accommodation. In Jersey, the German Army and Navy used the General Hospital in St. Helier, while the Air Force favoured the Merton Hotel. The *Hauptverbandsplatz* was manned on a care-and-maintenance basis by orderlies of the *319 Krankenwagen Kompanie* (319 Field Ambulance Company) and the female German Red Cross Nurses, who staffed the various *Soldatenheime* (Soldiers' Homes), had written orders instructing that, in the event of an enemy landing, they were to report immediately to the *Hauptverbandsplatz*. They were not on the permanent staff.

Was the hospital ever put to use? Travel writers wax eloquent on the subject, "... the Underground Hospital was very busy following the Allied landings in Normandy on D-Day, 1944," is the favourite line. This is obviously nonsense! The fighting front in France in June, 1944, was far too removed from the Channel Islands for the Germans to convey wounded troops all the way across Normandy to load them onto hospital ships bound for Jersey.

If the *Hauptverbandsplatz* had been used at all, it would have been during the siege of St. Malo in August, 1944, when many hundreds of wounded

Fig. 58 - One of the two main corridors pictured in the 1950s.
Société Jersiaise Photographic Archive, Jersey

Fig. 59 - The same view over 50 years later. ***Tony Pike***

troops were indeed brought to Jersey. Yet there is no evidence to suggest that any were tended inside *Ho 8*; soldiers were taken to the General Hospital where they littered the floors of the wards and corridors for days while they awaited treatment, while naval personnel were taken to the former *OT* Hospital at the Ladies' College which had been re-opened to receive them. It would seem that the *Hauptverbandsplatz* was kept in reserve for a direct attack upon Jersey.

With the cessation of hostilities *Ho 8* was handed over intact to Task Force 135 which liberated the Channel Islands, and was subsequently much visited and admired by experts of the British Army. Rather curiously, the first group of civilians to visit the complex after the Liberation consisted of members of the Jersey Green Room Club who were very fortunate to be able to include an official visit to the tunnel during their annual outing. The *Evening Post* of 23rd August 1945 carried a report of the visit submitted by the Club's secretary, Mrs. Ellen Le Feuvre, which is reproduced verbatim:–

Another most enjoyable and truly most interesting outing was organised by the social section of the Jersey Green Room Club for its members and their friends on August 21st.

This function took the form of a special visit to the German subterranean hospital at St. Peter's where the party of approximately 140 people was driven by charas; a military escort, under the able guidance of Capt. Sargent and his friends, conducted the party. After a brief explanatory speech made at the entrance, pointing out the wonderful engineering skill, labour and patience for this remarkable subterranean achievement, completely equipped with electricity, central heating, water supply and drainage, air conditioning facilities and telephone apparatus connecting every department of the hospital, Capt. Sargent headed the party through this amazing concreted structure; with its wide, lengthy corridors, innumerable general and private wards, closely packed with double tier beds separated by wooden stools; fitted with china wash basins, having hot and cold running water and telephone installation; also operating theatre, bath rooms, consulting rooms, mortuary, store rooms and kitchens complete with huge boilers, cookers, sinks and such like necessities.

It was eerie wandering through and getting lost among this maze of concrete corridors branching in all directions and terminating in another tunnel-like exit – delved out of the heart of pure Jersey granite. Such a place, being constructed under the pressure of sweated labour, and alas, taking toll of many lives, was undreamed of by Island inhabitants.

We are gratefully indebted to Capt. Sargent for this unique opportunity which will remain forever in our memory; this structure will also remain a symbol and grim reminder of the unforgettable five years.

Like many subsequent writers, Mrs. Le Feuvre was mistaken when she wrote that the tunnel was hewn out of "pure Jersey granite"; like most others, *Ho 8* was driven into the softer Brioverian shales.

As the work of clearing the Island of wartime artefacts progressed, so Captain (later Major) Sargent and his men stripped the tunnel of most of its furniture and fittings; what was not sold off at the many auction sales of former enemy equipment was doubtless dumped at sea. One item that did survive was the extremely large and useful electricity generator; first utilised at Overdale Hospital, it later became the standby generator at the General Hospital. When the latter establishment was rebuilt in the early 1980s, the generator was first donated to the Channel Islands Occupation Society and then, under an arrangement with the Public Works Department (which provided better entrance facilities at the Noirmont Command Bunker in exchange), was installed at Elizabeth Castle as a standby generator.

Fig. 60 - One of the hospital wards as it appeared in the 1950s, reflecting the bare state of the complex after the beds and other furniture had been stripped out.
Société Jersiaise Photographic Archive, Jersey

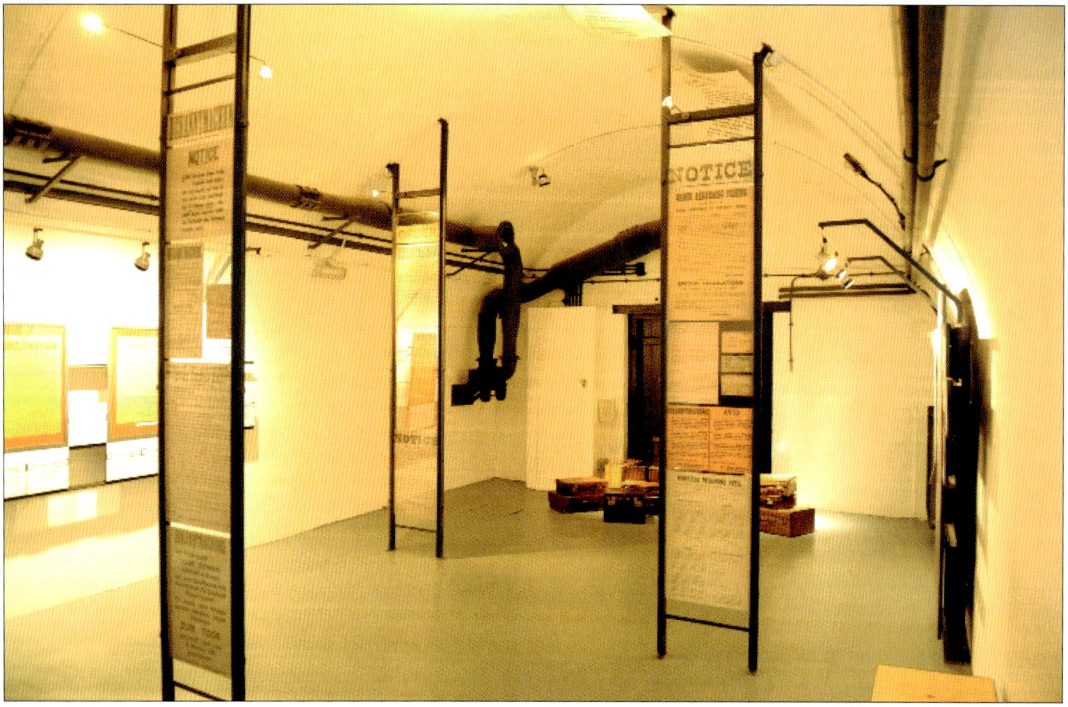

Fig. 61 - Today, the former wards are used as exhibition areas.
Tony Pike

By the first anniversary of Liberation Day on 9th May 1946, *Ho 8* was totally cleared and, in response to popular demand, opened to the public for the first time. By 2.00pm on the appointed day only a small group of people was waiting at the entrance to be shown around by military guides; this small group, however, did not portend what was to follow! On 10th May the *Evening Post* reported that:

When the doors opened the military, who were in charge, took parties of people on conducted tours of the tunnel and, as one party came out, another was let in. The number of those waiting, however, increased to such proportions that as far as the conducted tours were concerned the situation became uncontrollable and large numbers of people were in the building throughout the afternoon.

When the doors closed at 6.00pm a small number of people was waiting and had to be turned away. Traffic congestion on the roads approaching the hospital was great and cars were parked nose-to-tail for miles around the neighbouring countryside. Many of the later arrivals were forced to park their cars a mile or so from the hospital and walk the rest of the way. There was no charge for admission but a collecting box at the exit received a fair sum of money for military charities.

In the event, the sum of £69-6s-3d (£69.31) was collected and subsequently donated to the Jersey Branch of the British Legion. As for the enormous crowds which turned up, this was surely a case of coming events casting their shadows before them!

On 17th May 1946, the Lieutenant-Governor of Jersey, Lieut.-General Sir Edward Grassett, KB, DSO, (who was also General Officer Commanding Troops, Jersey) sent the following communication to Sir Alexander Coutanche, the Bailiff:–

I am now authorised by the War Office to state that all structures such as bakeries, ammunition tunnels, power stations and other

Fig. 62 - Although the gallery is lined with bricks rather than cement, this wartime (1944) view of a ward in Guernsey's Underground Hospital gives an accurate picture of how the Jersey equivalent would have looked at that time, with double-deck wooden beds and feeble lighting.
Royal Court/CIOS (Guernsey)

Fig. 63 - The escape shaft, which served as a chute for pouring liquid concrete during construction and where, it is claimed, a Spanish worker was fatally injured. ***Tony Pike***

fixed installations above and below ground in Jersey erected by the German occupying forces, other than those on WD land, will be handed over to the States of Jersey on 10th June, 1946, without charge, and full property rights will be vested in them.

Thus, in one fell swoop, the States of Jersey inherited large numbers of tunnels and other concrete structures; those which stood on private land, and for which they had no further use were sold off at minimal cost to the landowners, but others, such as *Ho 8*, which might be of future use, were retained.

The Department of Labour, under whose aegis came *Ho 8*, lost no time in opening the tunnel to the public, the first occasion being on 5th July 1946, and thereafter every Tuesday, Thursday and Sunday afternoon. Stripped of all furniture and fittings, all that was on view was the tunnel itself but in its genuine and original condition, unpainted and bare.

Nonetheless, the crowds turned up in droves on foot, by car and bus, while coaches queued up in what was then the narrow approach road on the Meadowbank side. In charge at the door was Mr. Jim Sutherland, an old soldier who had been employed as a foreman with the Department of Labour during the Occupation. With his splendid moustaches and a fresh flower in his buttonhole every day, he became as much of an institution as the tunnel complex itself; he retired in November, 1983, at the age of 84, and finally passed away in May, 1993 (the *Jersey Evening Post* issues for 2.9.83 and 19.11.83 refer).

Armed with nothing more than a table and a chair, a cash float and a roll of 6d. ($2\frac{1}{2}$p) tickets, Mr. Sutherland was on duty three afternoons a

Fig. 64 - Large sections of the uncompleted galleries lie in darkness and are inaccessible to the public, but some parts are visible, and have been used to create evocative displays. ***Tony Pike***

Fig. 65 - The cartoon which appeared in the *Evening Post* on 4th December 1961, following the handing over of the Underground Hospital, (dare we say it?) on a stretcher, to Daisy Hill Real Estates.
J. Mière Collection

week, on his own, throughout the summer. Then, after one season and on the grounds that everyone who would want to see the tunnel would have seen it by then, the Department of Labour decided to close down the operation, but Mr. Sutherland carried on opening the tunnel in his own time; the success of this voluntary deed convinced the Department that it was, after all, worth continuing and *Ho 8* was thereafter opened on a daily basis. The money rolled in!

When the Channel Islands Occupation Society conducts visitors around those bunkers which are in its care, the subject of *Ho 8* almost invariably raises its head. "Your island must make a mint out of those War Tunnels" is a comment frequently heard. In point of fact, however, all that Jersey probably makes out of *Ho 8* is the revenue accrued from income tax and parish rates, as the tunnel was acquired, free, gratis and for nothing, by a private company, said to be English-based, over 50 years ago. How could this be?

In 1960, Advocate Robert Vibert was handling the purchase of a plot of land situated over *Ho 8* from the Colonial Finance Company, for building purposes, on behalf of Daisy Hill Real Estates, a company owned by a Mr. John (later Sir John) Wills. The Advocate wondered by what right the States of Jersey occupied land beneath his client's property, as the rights of a landowner, under common law, state that he owns everything "*usque ad colecum, usque ad infernos*" ("to the heavens above and the depths below"). The Public Works Committee was asked: "By what right are you here?"

Public Works explained that the tunnel was handed over by HM Government as spoils of war and a gift to the Island. Advocate Vibert retorted

Fig. 66 - Jim Sutherland, Curator of the Underground Hospital from 1946 until his retirement in 1983. For the first 16 years he ran the place virtually single-handedly. *Jersey Evening Post*

that 'spoils of war' extended only to such things as tanks, guns, etc., and did not apply to real estate attached to the property of an individual. The Law Officers disagreed but Advocate Vibert persisted and eventually it had to be admitted that the War Office had given away what was not theirs to give.

Proceedings were instituted at the Cour d'Héritage in November, 1961, when Advocate Vibert challenged the Greffier of the States of Jersey to prove their title to the tunnel; this they could not do and so *Ho 8* was handed over to Daisy Hill, more or less on a plate, in a court hearing that lasted barely five minutes. Mr. Wills discovered that not only had he acquired a valuable piece of land but, at minimal extra cost, a nice little money earner beneath it!

By 1961, the sixpences paid in admission fees had netted the States some £33,000, a not inconsiderable sum in those days; in the heyday of the Jersey tourism industry in the 1970s and '80s an average of 300,000 people visited *Ho 8* every year, and although tourism numbers have declined in more recent years, the War Tunnels remain one of Jersey's top attractions.

The entire story is related in the book *Memoirs of a Jerseyman* (La Haule Books, 1992, Chapter XVI) by the late Senator Ralph Vibert, OBE, who kindly gave permission to quote from the relevant paragraphs, while articles in the *Evening Post* for 30th November and 2nd December 1961 also refer.

However, that was not the end of the story as Daisy Hill had failed to acquire the whole tunnel. Running right over the main Meadowbank entrance is the lane known as Les Charrières de Malorey, the property of the States and, as it is a bye-road, administered by the Parish of

Fig. 67 - Joe Mière, Assistant Curator for many years, and Curator from 1984 until his retirement in 1992. *Jersey Evening Post*

St. Lawrence; thus a narrow strip of the tunnel entrance still belonged to the States who could quite legally have barred access to visitors and, early in 1962, it looked as if they were going to do just that, having earlier acquired the land immediately around the entrance from the previous owner, a Mr. J. S. Romeril.

A situation had thus arisen whereby the States owned a few yards of tunnel giving them access to nowhere and Daisy Hill owned a vast complex without the right to use the main entrance. A case of sour grapes on the part of the States some said, and they could well have been right. Meanwhile, with the summer season approaching, Daisy Hill had to provide alternative access and announced that they would be developing the Cap Verd entrance, much to the alarm of the occupiers of the then newly erected houses at that spot, who could see car parks, toilets and snack bars springing up outside their prestigious properties, as the original facilities provided at the Meadowbank entrance would have been semi-redundant.

In the event, common sense prevailed; an annual wayleave was agreed upon, everybody was happy and things carried on as before (the *Evening Post* for 9.3.62 refers).

Ownership of the tunnel was eventually vested in a subsidiary of Daisy Hill Real Estates known as Sanctuary Inns Ltd. The displays inside *Ho 8* were greatly improved and during the winter of 1984/85, in time for the 40th anniversary of the Liberation, a massive refurbishment was put in hand, and the complex was renamed 'The German Military Underground Hospital - the Museum of the Occupation'.

In 2002, and under new management, a further refurbishment was put in hand, under the auspices of Messrs. Event Communications, when all the displays were reorganised, telling the story of the Occupation years under the title 'The Captive Isle'.

Fig. 68 - The rear (Cap Verd) entrance to *Ho 8* as it appeared early post-war – a view which remains practically unchanged (see front cover).
Société Jersiaise Photographic Archive, Jersey

In 2004 the name 'Underground Hospital' was dropped and the complex was re-branded as 'Ho 8 - Jersey War Tunnels' where, in addition to the exhibition in the tunnel itself, there is a well-run gift/book shop, a 'Garden of Reflection' and the 'War Trail' which meanders through nearby woods and takes in the site of an anti-aircraft battery.

Grands Vaux, St. Helier

***Ho 10*: Ration Store II** – North of the main valley road, between Le Mont Neron and Les Ruisseaux.

This tunnel curves through an elbow of rock lying between the two roads mentioned above. Known to Professor Klüpfel as the Mal Assis tunnel, the name being taken from the nearby water mill, the northern entrance of *Ho 10* lies in what used to be known as Bichard's Quarry; the quarry itself was filled in when the block of flats, 'Les Carrières', (i.e. 'The Quarries') was built in the 1960s. The concrete curve of the roof above the now blocked entrance may be seen protruding just above the surface of the car park to the rear of the flats.

The southern entrance lies beneath the immense rockfall that can be seen to the rear of the property known as 'Tangier'. The rubble removed during excavation was dumped in the meadow which lay across the road, on which was constructed the post-war Nicholson Park housing estate. The narrow gauge railway used for this task can be clearly seen on 1943 RAF aerial reconnaissance photographs, while the exact spot could, for many years, be pinpointed by the nicely repaired breach in the granite wall; however, this was breached again when 'Tangier' was built during the 1960s.

Ho 11 **: Personnel Shelter II** – Intended for excavation in the area of the dam of the Grands Vaux reservoir. Planning stage only.

Grands Vaux, St. Saviour

Ho 12 **: Fuel Store II** – The blocked entrance lies some 100 yards to the south of the road known as La Commune, where it descends from Victoria Village and joins La Rue au Bailli.

This tunnel is on private property and was under construction in mid-1943. However, the popular rumour that there is a "tunnel beneath Victoria Village" is false – only about 60 yards had been excavated when all work ceased; the contractor is thought to have been the firm of Olbricht. The adit was destroyed with explosives following the 1962 tragedy in *Ho 2*, but for many years the precise spot could be located by a length of prefabricated 60cm railway track protruding from the rock face. The track was recovered in 1980 and is now in the care of the Channel Islands Occupation Society.

Fig. 69 - The top of the sealed entrance to *Ho 10* may be seen just to the left of the notice boards in the car park behind Les Carrières Flats, Grands Vaux.

Le Mont au Roux, (La Haule Hill), St. Brelade

***Ho 14* : Fuel Store IV (Flak)** – Half-way up Le Mont au Roux, east side.

Lying on one of the roads leading to the Airport, this tunnel was intended for the use of the German Air Force (*Luftwaffe*). The possible location was in the enclave which lies roughly opposite the small reservoir half-way up the hill. Planning stage only.

Beaumont Valley, St. Peter

***Ho 13* : Munition Store IV (Flak)** – Beneath Beaumont Hill, just north of Warren Farm, on east side of the valley.

***Ho 15* : Stores** – Opposite Warren Farm, on west side of valley.

***Ho 16* : Personnel Shelter (?)** – Abandoned entrance on east side of Beaumont Hill, opposite the slope leading down to Warren Farm.

Few, if any, of the hundreds of motorists who daily rush up and down Beaumont Hill (La Route de Beaumont) realise that, on the one hand, they are driving past the entrance of an abandoned German tunnel and, on the other, driving over a largely complete one.

Little was known about these tunnels until Mrs. Margaret Long kindly made extracts from the diary of her late father, Mr. John Cutler Vincent, available to us; it is from this journal that more has been learnt about the day-to-day tunnelling activities of the *OT* than from any other source. As already mentioned, Mr. Vincent and his family lived in the house known as 'Lowlands' which stands at the lower end of Beaumont Valley and from where he ran a smallholding which was his livelihood; higher up the valley a Mr. Robert carried on a similar business from Warren Farm (still standing), and a Mr. Perrot operated from 'La Salmonerie', almost opposite and blown up in 1943. The valley itself was verdant and given over to orchards, potato fields, market gardening and grazing cattle.

Now it is time to say that here we encounter the first of the tunnels on the 'Meyer List'. This is *Ho 16*, but it does not appear on any of the known *Festpistab* maps; yet, as will be seen, there is a strong case for its existence. Similarly, the proposed use for *Ho 15* is open to doubt for, while it certainly appears on the July, 1943, *Festpistab* map, this does not include a listing of the tunnel's intended purposes; thus, this information for *Ho 15* is also taken from the Meyer List.

Mr. Vincent was an astute gentleman who noted everything mentally and committed most of this information to his diary. Once the excavations for the tunnels were in progress he kept a keen eye on "the Works" as he called them. On the odd Sunday when the workers had a day off, he would take his family up the valley to see how far the tunnels had progressed, even entering them in the early stages of construction with lighted matches for illumination.

He would regularly speak to the Spanish and French workers (and Russians as well when the opportunity arose) and constantly badgered the German overseers and engineers for information about "the Works" and what was intended – as well he might, for both he and his two neighbours lived under the constant threat of seeing their homes demolished.

The first intimation of coming events occurred on 8th July 1942, when Mr. Vincent was surprised to see a group of German surveyors arrive in the valley led by a young *Leutnant* of the German Air Force – this being an indication that the intended tunnels were to be for the use of the *Luftwaffe*. Surveying activities continued for some days and Mr. Vincent's opinion, from the nature of the surveying, was that a railway was to be laid up the valley (a correct assumption as it proved, but this did not materialise for another twelve months); some of the surveyors, however, were seen to be taking an interest in the valley slopes.

Nothing of consequence ensued during the month of August but, behind the scenes, the Fortress Engineers were busy! On 14th August they wrote to the *Feldkommandantur* (the German civilian administration) asking that the necessary land in Beaumont Valley be requisitioned for driving tunnels and the disposal of the spoil therefrom. However, the *Feldkommandant, Oberst* Knackfuss, was not too keen about the latter request, realising that the valley was important for the production of food for the military and civilians alike. Accordingly, the following reply was sent:–

Feldkommandantur 515
Military Admin. Group *Jersey 22.8.42*

To the:
Fortress Engineer Staff 14
Section 1a.

Subject:
Requisitioning of land for the construction of tunnels on the road system D11

I have sent my agricultural expert, Dr. Pelz, to inspect the above mentioned land lying to the west of Beaumont New Road (D11), on which you intend to dispose of the material removed from the proposed tunnels.

I ask you to abandon this plan as this section of land is far too valuable for the production of food to be used for the purpose which you propose. It seems possible for you to utilise the upper part of the valley which, in former times, the parochial authorities have already used for a rubbish dump and where, in any case, the valley is too narrow for agriculture.

This plea for common sense fell on deaf ears and it is obvious that the Fortress Engineers were able to ride rough shod over the wishes of the apparently almighty (to the civilian population, at any rate) *Feldkommandantur* when it suited them.

On 10th September Mr. Vincent's father (who lived at 'Oakhurst' on Beaumont Hill), told him

Fig. 70 - The abandoned entrance to the alleged *Ho 16* on Beaumont Hill.

Fig. 71 - During the short period of excavation of *Ho 16*, railway lines were set across the road, and projected over the valley on the left, on a girder pier; the spoil was dumped into Mr. Vincent's meadow below.

that he had been informed by the German surveyor that a tunnel would be driven into the hillside near his house (*Ho 16?*) and another (*Ho 13*) would be commenced in Robert's meadow in the valley. This is an illustration of how the tunnelling situation could change from month to month, for while the *Festpistab* map for May, 1942 only showed *Ho 13* being planned for Beaumont Valley, by September there is definite confirmation of two tunnels and on the 22nd of that month Spanish workers began delving into the eastern slopes of the valley, almost opposite 'Lowlands'; work here was abandoned a week later when they were unable to encounter a firm rock face.

Work actually commenced in the valley on 12th September when Mr. Vincent noted in his diary:–

... a big lorry stopped opposite Warren Farm, came down the steep slope and unloaded a big box and several wheelbarrows. About 10.00am between 40 and 50 Spaniards from the camp on the Marsh came up the hill and turned down Warren Farm lane, headed by an OT foreman. Their first job was to remove all the ground opposite Robert's pigsties and heap it at the bottom of the meadow. They left for dinner at 12.15 and arrived back at 1.15 ... they looked cheerful enough and do not appear to be obliged to hurry their work.

On 6th October, with work on the lower valley tunnel abandoned, the Spaniards began exploratory work into the slope near the driveway leading to 'Oakhurst' and Mr. Vincent guessed that this was the site for the tunnel at road level when, two days later, "... a drill started work to break up the surface of the road in preparation for a small railway track to cart the debris across the road." Again, two days later still, two tall wooden poles were erected in the bank just below Warren Farm, and these supported two stout steel girders which were laid horizontally from the level of the road. Mr. Vincent thought that "... this is for a continuation of the light railway coming across the road", the rails of which had by now been cemented into the surface of the roadway.

On 12th October, as predicted, the railway was extended out over the valley across the girders already mentioned; the operation provided a spot of light relief:–

... first the Spaniards appeared, each with a wooden sleeper which they dropped into place on the girders. Then more came along carrying a set of (prefabricated) railway track. With an OT foreman leading the way, carrying the rails with his hands behind him, and the Spaniards following, they worked their way cautiously across, from sleeper to sleeper, until, getting nervous, the Spaniards lowered their end leaving the OT man carrying his end alone. When he had put it down he followed the Spaniards and, waving his arms, shouted at them for nearly a minute.

Eventually, the job was completed and a side-tipping truck began removing spoil from the exploratory diggings and dumping it into Mr. Vincent's meadow. However, the same problem that had been encountered in the meadow repeated itself when no firm rock face could be found; on 28th October the German engineer from the tunnelling contractors (Heilmann & Littmann of Stuttgart) told Mr. Vincent that the road level tunnel had been abandoned and that work would commence on another tunnel on the west side of the valley. In passing, it may be mentioned that the rails laid across Beaumont Hill were removed on 31st October.

Fig. 72 - Every single item of building equipment used in connection with *Ho 13* and *Ho 15* was conveyed down the steep slope past Warren Farm.

This raises the question … was the tunnel at road level really *Ho 16*, or was it *Ho 15* with the latter number being transferred to the new tunnel in the valley when the former was abandoned? It is unlikely that we shall ever know the truth.

Although it will be out of chronological sequence to do so, it will be easier to describe *Ho 15* first before going on to the more complicated workings associated with *Ho 13*. Work on the definite *Ho 15* began on 21st November 1942, when Russians began clearing the ground for the northern entrance; work on the southern adit did not commence until 31st March 1943. These two pilot tunnels met on 18th May 1943, but, although the bore was widened, only the tunnel floor was concreted before work was abandoned in 1944.

However, it was *Ho 13* that occupied most of the space in Mr. Vincent's diary. By 17th September 1942 preliminary clearance work had commenced about 200 yards to the north of Warren Farm and by mid-October the pilot tunnel here was some 15 yards long but, because of water problems, was abandoned by the end of the month. A new adit was commenced nearer to Warren Farm on 4th November and another, some considerable distance to the north, a few days later – these are the two entrances that still survive. Problems with water were also encountered at the northern entrance and, even though the tunnellers persisted in this case, were sufficient to delay progress to the extent that this section was never lined and remains extremely dangerous to the present day.

Mr. Vincent's visits to "the Works" were curtailed on 29th November when tunnelling on a 24 hour, two shift arrangement, commenced; blasting took place roughly every 12 hours, once at tea time and again in the middle of the night. The excavations proceeded apace from both adits and the two headings were joined at 3.00pm on 25th March 1943.

Fig. 73 - The bricked-up lower entrance of *Ho 13*
Matthew Costard

In order to provide the compressed air necessary to work the pneumatic drills, the firm of Heilmann & Littmann was probably unique in Jersey in that it utilised steam engines to power the compressors rather than the more normal diesel engines. The first two such machines arrived on 18th September 1942, and were towed to the site, being on their own wheels and resembling the 'portable' type of engine normally used for threshing. They were positioned slightly to the north of Warren Farm and were enclosed in wooden sheds, where they were tended by Spanish mechanics. The compressed air produced by the machines was stored in a tall vertical, cylindrical reservoir tank.

Water for the engines' boilers was supplied from a concrete reservoir erected in 'Perrot's Valley', opposite Warren Farm (still standing in 2012) and the water was carried across to the engines by means of a metal pipe, supported on posts, about ten feet above the valley floor.

A third engine had arrived by November, but this was non-portable and had to be erected on a concrete platform. By 5th November a wooden tower was in the course of construction close to the engines and eventually it became clear that this was, in fact, scaffolding to facilitate the erection of a fifty foot high chimney to take the exhaust smoke and steam from all three engines. However, none of the engines was exactly in the first flush of youth, having all been built before the First World War by the firm of R.Wolf, Buckau, Magdeburg. In the opening months of 1943, they were constantly giving trouble – at one stage all three were broken down and had to be dismantled; a diesel compressor was brought in as a stopgap.

On 11th January 1943, a boiler for a fourth, even larger, engine arrived and was parked temporarily in the entrance of the abandoned *Ho 16*, the remainder of the engine arriving on 7th February. With enormous 10½ feet diameter twin fly-wheels, it was eventually assembled but did not begin work until July or August.

Mr. Vincent was a keen observer of the workers and spoke to them whenever possible. He noted that they came from two camps - *Lager Schepke* on Goose Green Marsh and *Lager Udet* at La Moye. Those from the latter camp arrived at 7.00am packed into a lorry and were taken away in the same manner at the end of their shift unless, when there was a fuel shortage and work ended earlier, they would be marched back to camp by way of Le Mont des Vignes and La Route des Quennevais.

Not all workers laboured at the rock face – Mr. Vincent noted that one Russian followed his trade as a blacksmith and another carted coal with a wheelbarrow for the steam engines. Yet another had one of the easiest jobs of all – he gathered clay which he formed into balls and these were used to

Fig. 74 - The lower entrance of *Ho 15* as it appeared in the 1990s.

Fig. 75 - The lower end of the culvert erected to cover the stream running down Beaumont Valley. Some idea of the height of the culvert can be gained from the fact that the late Robin Cox, standing alongside, was slightly over 6 feet tall himself. The presence of this culvert led to post-war stories that it was part of a ramp to launch flying bombs against England!

pack the shot holes for the gelignite when blasting. On 23rd June 1943, he noted "… we have noticed lately how much harder the Russians are working; there is little slacking now. One has heard that they are better fed; they are certainly better dressed." On another occasion he saw an *OT* overseer strike a Russian with the handle of a long shovel, so hard that the blow was audible and the recipient had to have his head bandaged as a result; afterwards, "… he came back to work."

On 16th June 1943, Mr. Vincent noted that "… two Spaniards were injured in one of the tunnels today and the German Red Cross ambulance went up to fetch them."

On 2nd May 1943, Mr. Vincent was greatly intrigued by "… a big new erection – a high bridge towering 20 feet above Beaumont Hill, jutting out over the valley and reaching up into Syvret's late potato field above the hill."

An explanation was forthcoming seven days later:–

The German Manager has explained the purpose of the mysterious wooden bridge across the New Hill. Its north east end reaches about halfway up Syvret's late potato patch and this spot is exactly above the centre of the semi-circular tunnel, the two borings of which met on 25th March. A hole or shaft will be made into the field to reach the tunnel below. A cement mixer is already in position in Robert's meadow, against the bank, and just under the south-west end of the bridge. Cement will be hoisted up this end, run along the bridge and dropped through the hole in the field to the workers below in the tunnel. The next plan is to cement the interior of the tunnel. Nobody knows why the prepared cement cannot be carted into the tunnel the normal way by which all the excavated stones are removed. What a lot of cement will be wasted!

This method of working was adopted to expedite construction and avoided the wet cement going in, clashing with the excavated stone coming out. The bore of the tunnel was widened from the centre of the tunnel outwards and the final lining followed the same course. The "hole or shaft" was, of course, the embryo escape shaft. Sand (from the beach at Grève de Lecq), and gravel for the aggregate, was delivered by lorry at road level into three "huge concrete bins" which stood adjacent to the mixer on the valley floor.

The biggest worry for Mr. Vincent and his neighbours was the stone excavated from the two tunnels. In defiance of the wishes of the *Feldkommandant* that the productive valley be spared, the *OT* dumped (as was their usual practice) all the spoil onto the valley floor, not only gradually obliterating the fields, orchards and meadows but, worse still, threatening the three houses mentioned earlier. It was also necessary to construct a concrete culvert into which the fast flowing stream had to be diverted in order to avoid flooding.

The first indications of this culvert were to be seen on 28th November 1942, when another surveying team arrived on site. In response to Mr. Vincent's query as to whether a railway was to be laid, the German surveyor replied "*Nein, ein Kanal*". Work on the culvert commenced on 18th December at the upper end of the valley and proceeded southwards but it did not precisely follow the original course of the stream. Once construction was well under way, the 60cm gauge railway emerging from the mouth of *Ho 13* was laid across the meadow, supported off the ground on a wooden trestle. Trains consisting of up to seven tipping wagons, drawn by a small diesel locomotive, dumped the rubble onto the once verdant meadow, inexorably raising the level of the valley floor and gradually creeping down towards the three dwellings.

Despite the fact that all three families were under notice to quit in due course, the only one on which the blow actually fell was Perrot at 'La Salmonerie'. On 31st December 1942, they were warned that they would have to abandon their home and livelihood; they actually moved out on 26th January 1943, the Constable of St. Peter having found alternative accommodation for them at 'Beaulieu' on nearby Old Beaumont Hill. On 13th March Mr. Vincent recorded that "... the demolition of Perrot's house is proceeding. The roof has gone. Yesterday they were knocking the slates inwards."

Then, on 25th March:–

Dad called out to say that Mr. P's house would soon be blown up. I went to the top of the avenue to see ... there was only the shell of the place left ... lengths of electric cables were in evidence and men put sheets of corrugated iron against the bottom windows of Warren Farm ... at 5.00pm there was a great noise. All we could see for some time was a great cloud of dust. When this had cleared, it revealed that the house had collapsed.

Fearful that a similar fate would overtake 'Lowlands', Mr. Vincent had already invited the German engineer into his home on 2nd January 1943, in order to learn the worst. He was told that he was safe until May or June at the earliest as, due to a shortage of labourers, the work was behind schedule. By August, the Vincent family was still in residence and no further word had been received regarding the loss of their property. In fact, fate had intervened and the house had been reprieved but they were not to learn of this for another four or five weeks.

Meanwhile, the railway had reared its head again. On 14th March 1943, loads of rails and sleepers began to be delivered to the "pier" which still protruded above Mr. Vincent's meadow, opposite the abandoned *Ho 16*. These were dumped into the meadow and left for the time being. On 28th June an elderly *OT* officer appeared at Mr. Vincent's front door and explained that a railway was to be laid up his lane and that the end of the horse stable would have to come down; meanwhile, some Spaniards and Jerseymen had begun to hack down trees and bushes that were in the way. An "animated discussion" broke out when a neighbour, a Mr. Hall, had ordered them to stop as they had no Requisition Order.

Mr. Hall was not the only one to complain! On about 5th July Mr. Raulin de la Haye, who owned Brocklyn Farm in La Ruelle ès Ruaux, to the south of 'Lowlands', had appeared at the *Feldkommandantur* in St. Helier complaining loudly that the *OT* was about to lay a railway through his farmyard, demolishing his two most important outbuildings in the process, and what did the *Feldkommandant* intend to do about it?

The *Feldkommandantur* wrote immediately to the *OT* asking if this was correct as this was the first that they had heard about the railway. The *OT* replied that, yes, this was correct and they had been asked by the *Festpistab*, in response to a request from the *Luftwaffe* Construction Section, to connect the Beaumont Valley tunnels to the main metre gauge railway system.

All this became evident to Mr. Vincent on 7th July when he recorded that "... we hear that the German Authorities are examining the railway plan to try to avoid de la Haye's stables." And again on 15th July "... the *Kommandant* himself, Colonel Knackfuss, came out this week to see about the proposed railway."

Mr. de la Haye's protests eventually bore fruit when the *Feldkommandant* ordered the *OT* to think again and move the railway as the farm was important for the production of food. The outcome was recorded on 27th July:–

Disturbed just before lunch by small party of OTs coming up Andrew's meadow into our field

Fig. 76 - The year is 1939 and the old copper mines beneath Westmount, St. Helier, are being re-opened for use as air raid shelters. If the fellow with the sledge hammer misses his target, the young man holding the chisel is in for a nasty accident! *Jersey Evening Post*

with their red and white marking poles. The German was the OT officer Captain Sholt (so his Jerseyman interpreter told me) … we learned that the original idea of a railway up our lane was scrapped, thanks to Raulin de la Haye who had protested about it going through his stables. Instead it will come through part only of his land, through the upper part of Moignard's meadow …

In the event, the entire exercise proved to be academic. On 6th September Mr. Vincent's diary records "… saw the German manager reading out a paper to a group of workers; apparently the firm of Heilmann & Littmann are to send all their workers to the Calais area, leaving only six or so key men and all the Russians." Eventually, he learnt that even the Russians were to go and, on 29th September, he wrote "… the firm of Heilmann & Littmann are packing up in earnest. Several sheds have been taken down, including the office, and two of the engine sheds are already gone."

By 9th October the bridge over the road had gone, the steam engines had been dismantled and "… the big chimney was unbolted and fell with a crash in a westerly direction." On the following day the Russians turned up for work as usual in the morning but at 2.30pm they boarded a bus and left for the Harbour en route for France. The same afternoon, it being a Sunday, the Vincent family "… walked up the Hill to see the desolation of the Works."

Meanwhile, on 2nd October, a caravan-like shed on wheels had arrived together with a gang of Jersey, Irish and Spanish workers who proved to be employees of Elsche. These assisted with the dismantling of the plant and in the middle of the month commenced to brick up the entrances to *Ho 13* and, later, to lay a concrete floor inside *Ho 15*.

Thereafter, with his house and living reprieved, Mr. Vincent's diary ceases to mention Beaumont Valley and "the Works" but there can be no doubt whatsoever that the value of his contribution to our knowledge of the tunnelling cannot be overstated.

After the war the bungalow 'St. Ives' was erected more or less on the site of 'La Salmonerie' but otherwise the upper end of Beaumont Valley has lain dormant. An idea of the depth of the culvert housing the brook can be gained by lifting the wooden cover to one of the brick built inspection chambers thoughtfully provided by the *OT*; the water can be heard thundering some 12 feet below. Other inspection shafts, brick built and some ten feet high, are to be seen dotted around over the track of the culvert lower down the valley.

For some years part of the lined section of *Ho 13* was used for water storage, but both entrances have now been sealed. *Ho 15* is also inaccessible; the northern entrance has been buried and the southern entrance secured with a padlocked gate.

Westmount, St. Helier
Ho 18 (?) : Hospital – Planning stage only.

Here is another of the tunnels on the 'Meyer List' which, it has to be said, has a ring of authenticity about it for two reasons. First, although the *Festpistab* maps for Jersey do not show a hospital on the list of planned tunnels, those for Guernsey and Alderney do; thus there is no reason to suppose that Jersey would have been any different and would eventually have had a tunnel dedicated for the purpose rather than the converted *Ho 8* which was, in fact, the case.

Secondly, it is a little known fact that a pilot tunnel was bored into the lower slopes of Westmount in the 19th Century in the belief that the rock thereabouts was suitable for the mining of copper. When these hopes were dashed the tunnel was sealed, but re-opened in 1939 by the Parish of St. Helier, fitted with wooden benches, and made available for use as an air raid shelter. The tunnel was situated about half-way

Fig. 77 - Seats and lighting were provided inside the old mine adits for shelterers. If the 'Meyer List' is correct, the Germans were going to develop these old workings into *Ho 18*, the original 'underground hospital'. *Jersey Evening Post*

up the hill, almost opposite the Bowling Club headquarters, and would most likely have become *Ho 18* had work ever commenced.

Thus, not only would the Germans have had their work started for them, but the proposed *Ho 18* would have been conveniently situated beneath Overdale Hospital and not far from the rear entrance of the General Hospital in Kensington Place as well.

Again, *Ho 18* is one of those minor mysteries to which we will doubtless never find the answer.

La Folie, St. Helier

_Ho 19_: Harbour Electricity Generating Station – Under construction.

_Ho 20_(?) : Mount Bingham Connecting Tunnel – Under construction(?)
Eastern Railway Tunnel – Completed and in operation.

This group of tunnels lies close to St. Helier Harbour, between La Folie Inn and the South Pier, burrowing beneath Mount Bingham. For ease of description of certain events, it will be opportune to deal with the railway tunnel first.

On 15th July 1942, the *OT*, with due pomp and circumstance as befits such an occasion, opened their metre gauge steam railway which was to carry vast quantities of building material and supplies to the west of the Island, although at the time of the opening it was stated that this railway would eventually run to all parts of Jersey. However, when surveying the route to serve the east of the Island, it was not long before the *OT* came up against Le Mont de la Ville (on which stands Fort Regent), the one obstacle that thwarted the 19th Century railway promoters and their plans to lay a railway from St. Aubin in the west to St. Catherine in the east.

Fig. 78 - The entrances to *Ho 19* (left), and the *OT* eastern railway tunnel which was built on the 'cut-and-cover' principle.

Consequently, when the time came to lay the railway to the east in 1943, the route chosen took the line along Commercial Buildings, through the then Harbour Works Yard (now the site of the Jersey Electricity Company's power station) and around the walks at La Collette. This route dictated that a narrower gauge of 60cm had to be used, a wooden bridge had to be built across the French Harbour at La Folie, and a tunnel excavated beneath Mount Bingham.

First mention of the railway tunnel is contained in Sinel's *Diary* when, on 26th May 1943, he wrote:

... Blasting has been going on at the end of the Victoria Pier, near the Harvey Monument; this is in connection with the tunnel which has been bored under Mount Bingham for the railway to run through. In today's operations a large part of the wall coping on the top road was blown away and will have to be replaced.

Those who have memories of this happening all relate the incident with relish, assuming that the *OT* had placed too great a charge in position and accidentally blown up the roadway. This, however, was not the case; the blowing up of the road had been planned well in advance, the *OT* having written the following letter to the *Feldkommandantur* on 29th April 1943:–

Subject: Eastern Railway Tunnel.

The Organisation Todt is building a 60cm gauge railway from St. Helier Harbour to Gorey. This is in preparation for the fortifications works to be built in the east. For this purpose work has begun at Victoria Pier to drive a tunnel through the sharply projecting rock salient.

It now appears that the stone in the tunnel below Pier Road is very fissured and that it will not be possible, with the means available, to complete this tunnel by normal mining methods. Additionally, in view of the fissuring, the roof of the tunnel will be too thin after the final cross section has been cut, to continue to bear the weight of the traffic above. We shall therefore be obliged to complete this section of about 15 metres in length by opencast working.

It is therefore necessary for this purpose that the section of Pier Road from Victoria Pier to the first curve on Mount Bingham should be closed to traffic for about three weeks in order to be able to build the tunnel.

I therefore request that Pier Road be closed to traffic during the period 2nd to 23rd May, 1943.

The Section Construction Chief
(signed) Grienberg
Administrative Building Adviser

The German military always took a serious view of road closures as such measures impeded their operations but, nevertheless, in this case, permission was duly granted. However, subsequent events dictated that the fissured rock of Mount Bingham would lead to further, unplanned, road closures some seven months later. (It would be relevant to add here that the same fissured rock of Le Mont de la Ville was also destined to cause problems for the contractors constructing the Fort Regent road tunnel in 1969).

Thus, like the Metropolitan Railway in London, the railway tunnel beneath Mount Bingham was completed using the 'cut-and-cover' method of construction and it still survives today carrying the high tension cables of the Jersey Electricity Company from La Collette power station to other parts of the Island, the smoke blackened ceiling bearing witness to the passage of both steam and diesel locomotives over 65 years ago.

The 'Meyer List' numbers this tunnel as "*Ho 20* – Mount Bingham Connecting Tunnel", but it is our opinion that if there was indeed an *Ho 20*, it was far more likely to have been an extension of *Ho 19*, as will be explained in a moment.

Ho 19 is another of those enigmas presented by the *Festpistab* map of 1942. The map dated 1st June 1942, gives no indication whatsoever of any intention to bore a tunnel at La Folie, yet, on 31st July 1942, Leslie Sinel records that "among the many blasting operations which are taking place is a huge tunnel being made at the bottom of the Victoria Pier under Mount Bingham."

This tunnel is shown on the July, 1943, map and it was *Ho 19*, the Harbour Electricity Generating Station; although constructed by the *OT* firm of Riechert (replaced in March, 1943, by another firm, namely Hellenbart), *Ho 19* was under the supervision of the *Marinehafenbauamt Kanalinseln, Abteilung Jersey*, (Naval Harbour Construction HQ, Channel Islands, Jersey Section) which had its offices at No. 4 Commercial Buildings, little more than a stone's throw from *Ho 19*, in fact.

One of the biggest fears of the German Navy was that a few well aimed bombs descending upon the Queen's Road power station of the Jersey Electricity Company (JEC) would render every crane in St. Helier Harbour useless. With this in mind, a number of steam powered cranes was 'borrowed' from the French port of Rouen and installed upon the New North Quay. These, however, were only a stopgap and it was decided that the best solution was to place a small power station, for the exclusive use of the cranes, in a tunnel close to the Harbour – hence *Ho 19*.

Between the months of August and November, 1942, considerable correspondence shuttled to and fro between the *Hafenbauamt* and the *Feldkommandantur* concerning the installation of an electric motor in the tunnel and the supply of the necessary fuel to the Jersey Electricity Company at Queen's Road, from whence the power to operate the motor would emanate. The surviving correspondence shows how the German authorities went into precise detail over such matters!

Fig. 79 - The interior of the eastern railway tunnel.

The advice of the Manager of the JEC was sought and he calculated that the planned operation of the 17 kilowatt motor for 14 hours per calendar day (420 hours per month) would produce 7,140 kilowatts per month. As it required 450 grams of diesel to produce one kilowatt, the total fuel consumption for one month would be 3,213 kgs., or 3.213 metric tonnes. The Riechert Company was instructed by the *Feldkommandantur* to supply (via the *Hafenbauamt*) the JEC with 10 tonnes, or 12,000 litres, of diesel oil so that they could generate the current to power the motor for three months.

By 30th October the motor had not been installed as the *Hafenbauamt* was unable to supply the necessary fuel to the JEC so that, on 21st November, the *Feldkommandantur* reluctantly agreed to provide the diesel from its own stocks. However, it was stipulated that the motor was not to be operated during the hours of peak electricity consumption, i.e. from 7.00 to 9.00am, and 5.00 to 9.00pm, and that the current consumed had to be metered.

Again, on 30th October, it was recorded that two diesel powered MAN generators, with a combined output of 450 kilowatts, had arrived for eventual installation in *Ho 19*, and that completion of the tunnel was scheduled for twelve months' time. Because of this delay, the two MAN machines must have been put to work elsewhere as another source records that, in 1943, two French generators had arrived; these, however, had been sabotaged at the Renault factory where they had been made. It required the services of a French mechanic, working voluntarily for the *OT*, to strip the motors completely and remove the sand with which they had been filled!

Progress, however, was slow and by October, 1943, when the bulk of the *OT* had left Jersey, and all work on the tunnel had ceased, *Ho 19* had only been excavated in rough form, no concrete lining having been installed whatsoever. This was due to the fact that the contractors had had to contend with the "good, solid, Jersey granite" so beloved by the guide book writers and not the softer Brioverian shales through which most of the other tunnels were driven.

However, in November, 1943, the problem with the fissured rock in this area, foreseen some six months earlier in connection with the excavation of the adjacent railway tunnel, once again reared its head. At the point where *Ho 19* enters the rock face at La Folie, the unavoidably thin 'crust' of the tunnel roof had to bear the weight of much heavy military traffic passing along Pier Road and it began to show signs of wear and tear. Accordingly, the decision was taken to line the entrance of *Ho 19* in order to strengthen that portion of the roof which had to bear the weight of this traffic and, on 18th November 1943, the *Feldkommandantur* was advised that it would be necessary to close Pier Road once again for a period of about one month.

The ubiquitous Theodore Elsche and his workforce of local voluntary labour was given the task of installing the lining and, as in the case of the railway tunnel, the road surface was destroyed; wooden shuttering was erected inside the tunnel and the concrete mixers placed overhead in the roadway, the wet concrete being poured directly from the mixers onto the formwork below. As speed was of the essence, work forged ahead night and day with floodlights being used during the hours of darkness; these were switched off whenever Allied aircraft were passing overhead, en route to France.

The lining was built up to within two feet of the road surface and this was covered with a layer of pitch to waterproof the concrete beneath. More concrete was then poured to make good the road surface and the resulting white patch showed up in every subsequent RAF aerial reconnaissance photograph; indeed, it remained very evident, as did the cover of the nearby railway tunnel, until the road was resurfaced sometime in the 1950s.

With the entrance to *Ho 19* made secure, all work then appears to have been abandoned and the tunnel left in the same condition as it is today. Inside, on the right (or south side) is the large chamber which would have housed the generators, while a pilot tunnel stretches off in an easterly direction for several hundred yards, the extremity being somewhere beneath the children's play area on Mount Bingham. From this pilot tunnel, another branch strikes off in a north-easterly direction.

Here, the matter of the alleged *Ho 20*, the Mount Bingham Connecting Tunnel included in the 'Meyer List', rears its head. If *Ho 19* was intended to be an electricity generating station, all that it would require would have been two large chambers, one for the generators and one for fuel tanks; it surely would have not needed two long galleries stretching off into the far distance. It is these galleries that lend credence to the theory that

Fig. 80 - The lined section of *Ho 19* beneath Pier Road.

Fig. 81 - The incomplete chamber for the generating plant – although fairly dry when the tunnel was surveyed by the CIOS in the 1990s, there are now several inches of water covering the floor.
Steve Powell

Ho 20 was planned as an extension of *Ho 19* to enable troops and material to pass from one side of Mount Bingham/South Hill to the other without having to appear above ground. *Ho 20* was hardly likely to have been the nearby railway tunnel which, in any case, was not strictly a tunnel at all, but a passage constructed in concrete. Again, we shall never know the truth.

For many years after the war *Ho 19* was used as a loading point for the road tankers of the JEC conveying fuel for the generators at the Queen's Road power station. The tankers would reverse into the tunnel entrance and be filled from a pipeline in the roof which ran from the nearby oil storage tanks. With the opening of La Collette power station the need to transport fuel oil across St. Helier ceased and today *Ho 19* is used as a store by the Transport and Technical Services Department. By way of conclusion, it should be mentioned that the rubble from *Ho 19* was used to build up the track bed of the 60cm gauge railway to the east over part of the Old Harbour and along the foreshore at La Collette.

Le Mont du Jubilé (Jubilee Hill), St. Peter

***Ho 21* (?) : Stores (?)** – Planned, but abandoned.

The fact that this tunnel was planned is not in dispute, for not only is it mentioned in Professor Klüpfel's diary, but a sketch in his field note book pinpoints its location to have been opposite the bend about half-way down Jubilee Hill and on the south side of the road. According to the Professor, work was abandoned owing to water problems near the proposed entrance. The abandonment must have been decided at an early date because the tunnel does not even appear on the May, 1942 *Festpistab* map.

Fig. 82 - The parting of the ways in the eastern extension of *Ho 19* (or is it *Ho 20*?) *Steve Powell*

What is in question, however, is the designated number, which comes from the 'Meyer List', as well as the intended purpose. 'Stores' is somewhat ambiguous, especially when one considers that the *Festpistab* maps are much more explicit when detailing the purposes of all the other tunnels. Bearing in mind the proximity of this tunnel to the Airport, it could well have been intended as an equipment store and workshop for the *Luftwaffe*; a similar tunnel was planned for this purpose in Guernsey in the area of Le Bourg, close to the Airport in that island.

Rozel Valley, St. Martin
Ho 22 (?) : Stores – Planning stage only (?)

This tunnel, even at the planning stage, is suspect, being taken from the 'Meyer List'; it is true that there would be every reason to have a munition store in the east of the Island but the only evidence of its existence, like that of the three following tunnels, comes from Herr Meyer, the former *OT* official, who supplied details to Joe Mière from memory.

Grouville Marsh, Grouville
Ho 23 (?) : Personnel Shelter – Planning stage only (?)

It being obviously impossible to construct a tunnel in a marsh, the most likely location for this tunnel would have been at the nearby Les Maltières Quarry, a few hundred yards to the west of Gorey Village. Again from the 'Meyer List', *Ho 23* must remain suspect until some firm primary source confirming its planned location can be found.

Grève de Lecq Valley, St. Mary/ St. Ouen
Ho 24 & *25* (?) : Stores – Under construction but sealed (?)

According to Herr Meyer, *Ho 24* and *Ho 25* were under construction but were sealed at the end of the war; he even provided a rough sketch plan of their layout.

Frankly, there is no physical evidence whatsoever

Fig. 83 - The remains of the ventilation trunking still in position. ***Steve Powell***

Fig. 84 - ... as well as supports for electricity cables. ***Steve Powell***

to suggest that these tunnels were under construction. Had they been so, to the extent that the sketch plans suggest, then the rubble extracted would have obliterated the floor of Grève de Lecq Valley in the same manner as all the other valleys were desecrated wherever tunnels were constructed. Nor do any of the many aerial reconnaissance photographs taken by the RAF reveal any evidence whatsoever of tunnels under construction.

Fig. 85 - Looking up from the foot of the stairs which lead down to the interior of *Ho Etacquerel.*

L'Etacq, St. Ouen

Ho Etacquerel – Completed. Defensive tunnel forming part of *Stützpunkt Etacquerel* (Strongpoint *Etacquerel*).

Due to the fact that it is tucked away behind a frontage consisting of a standard Type 670 (*Regelbau 670*) casemate for a *10,5cm K 331(f)* coastal defence gun almost opposite Mariner Cottages at L'Etacq, there is no external evidence whatsoever that this tunnel exists. Yet exist it most certainly does and burrows back into the hillside for some distance, curving to the left and ending in a substantial flight of stairs which lead up to the main entrance situated behind the large private house built on the site of the former L'Etacquerel Hotel.

Fig. 86 - The entrance to the complex, which had been concealed by a post-war garage, was exposed when the site was redeveloped in 2002.

Fig. 87 - The 'business end' of *Ho Etacquerel*, opposite Mariner Cottages at L'Etacq. The gun was removed during the 1953 scrap metal drive.

Fig. 88 - The central heating system. Nearby is a small cooking range.

Fig. 89 - The main corridor at *Ho Etacquerel*. Note the concrete-work of the curved roof section.

The tunnel not only incorporates accommodation for personnel and ammunition, but includes a central heating system, cooking facilities, ventilation plant, and a generator. Unfortunately, due to neglect, much of the metalwork is rusting away. If permission can be obtained, this tunnel is well worth a visit.

Verclut Point, St. Martin (St. Catherine's Breakwater)

Ho Mole Verclut – Forms part of *Widerstandsnest Mole Verclut* (Resistance Nest *Mole Verclut*).

Verclut Point is the correct geographical name for the area popularly known as St. Catherine's Breakwater, the latter name always being studiously ignored by the Germans on their defensive maps. In the 19th Century the British Government authorised the construction of a massive naval base at this point. Work commenced in 1847 but, after ten years' hard toil which saw the completion of one arm only of the harbour – the 'Breakwater' – the project was abandoned (see *The Harbour that Failed* by W. Davies, Ampersand Press 1983).

Stone for the construction of the Breakwater was quarried on the spot, leaving a large 'island' of isolated rock which has come to be known as 'Gibraltar' due to its resemblance to the Rock of Gibraltar at the entrance to the Mediterranean. However, opinions on this differ, some saying that the name has been transferred from the area near St. Catherine's crossroads which, in turn, has taken its name from the nearby Gibraltar Farm.

Whatever the truth of the matter the Germans seized upon Gibraltar as an ideal location to site a defensive tunnel equivalent to *Ho Etacquerel* at the opposite end of the Island, although not nearly as substantial. Consisting of a single tunnel with two side chambers, one completed and the other half-finished, *Ho Mole Verclut* curves through Gibraltar from a simple entrance door and ends in another standard Type 670 casemate housing a *10,5cm K 331(f)* coastal defence gun which covered the length of the Breakwater.

Ho Mole Verclut is obviously a victim of the run

Fig. 90 - The so-called 'Gibraltar Rock' at St. Catherine's Breakwater in 1945, with the rear entrance to *Ho Mole Verclut* nestling at the foot. Note the enormous length of the ventilation intake pipe.
Jersey Evening Post

Fig. 91 - A wartime (1944) view of the *10,5cm K 331(f)* coastal defence gun at *Ho Mole Verclut.*
CIOS Collection

Fig. 92 - At the commencement of the tunnel behind the gun room, the walls and ceiling are lined in plaster and brick. ***Richard Perchard***

Fig. 93 - Further inside, and only the walls are lined with a coarse mix of gravel and cement. ***Richard Perchard***

Fig. 94 - At the outer extremity, the tunnel is totally unlined.
Richard Perchard

down of the fortification programme in October, 1943, as it is far from complete; the bore of the tunnel was first lined with a coarse skim of cement mixed with gravel gathered from the beach in the vicinity and stone from Les Maltières Quarry at Gorey, but containing no sand whatsoever. This coarse lining was in the process of being covered with cement bricks when all work on the tunnel ceased. The use of brickwork suggests that construction was in the hands of the Army Rock Drilling Company rather than the *OT*, as the same method of lining was used by this unit inside the defensive tunnel at *Stützpunkt Doktorhaus* situated at Mont Matthieu, St. Ouen (see below).

Apart from an interval in the 1990s *Ho Mole Verclut* has housed a vivier for the storage of live shellfish; permission was sought to convert the complex into an aquarium and marine study centre, with the inevitable restaurant, but thankfully this was refused.

Mont Matthieu, St. Ouen

Stützpunkt Doktorhaus – Defensive tunnel forming a personnel shelter for the troops of Strongpoint *Doktorhaus*.

Protruding onto the hill known as Mont Matthieu, which leads out of St. Ouen's Bay, is a bunker incorporating two defensive machine-gun loopholes and, uniquely for Jersey, displaying the title of the unit that built it, namely *Gesteinsbohr Komp 77*, or Rock Drilling Company 77. To be strictly accurate, it was actually the 4th Company of Rock Drilling Battalion 77 that carried out the work; this was an Army Construction unit that came to Jersey at the end of 1941 and departed in mid-July, 1943.

What the casual passer-by cannot know is that concealed behind the bunker is a tunnel forming a personnel shelter for the troops manning the adjacent strongpoint; this derived its name by association with the nearby property known as

Fig. 95 - Strongpoint *Doktorhaus*: Paul Burnal studies the legend on the bunker (marked 'A' on the plan on page 121), which covers the entrance to the tunnel on Mont Matthieu.

'La Rocque Onvoy'. Built in the 1930s, this house was owned by a Dr. Evans; with sweeping views over St. Ouen's Bay, it was an obvious choice for the Germans to use it as a headquarters, ultimately for the 3rd Company of Machine-Gun Battalion 16, the unit which defended that part of the Island.

Fig. 96 - Looking up the tunnel stairs towards the entrance.

With a wry sense of humour, they lost no time in naming the strongpoint which grew up on the opposite side of the road, where the post-war housing development known as Bay View Court stands, as *Stützpunkt Doktorhaus*. In addition to defending the exit from St. Ouen's Bay, this position provided mobile troops whose task was to wait in a secure shelter during the initial phase of an amphibious assault, only to emerge if the landing was successful and enemy troops began to move inland. The tunnel runs through the hillside for a few score yards, not only incorporating chambers for personnel, weapons and ammunition, but giving direct access, by means of a lengthy iron runged ladder, to the massively constructed Company command and observation position which stands on the edge of the escarpment running behind the bay.

Fig. 97 - The immaculate brick lining of the tunnel's interior.

Fig. 98 - Close-up of the plaque reading '*Gesteinsbohr. Komp. 77*' (Rock Drilling Battalion 77).

Fig. 99 - One of the accommodation chambers now converted into water storage tanks.

Fig. 100 - The command and observation post of Strongpoint *Doktorhaus* which stands in the grounds of Bay View Court (marked 'B' on the plan).

La Corbière, St. Brelade

Stützpunkt Corbiere – Communication tunnel connecting two bunkers on the north side of the road leading down to the lighthouse.

Fig. 101 - Strongpoint *Corbiere*: the stairway in the *M19* mortar bunker leading down to the communication tunnel.

It was common practice in Jersey for every bunker within a strongpoint or resistance nest to be self-standing, so that if one fell to the enemy others within the complex would not necessarily follow suit. In direct defiance of this principle, and lying just to the north of the road leading to the lighthouse at La Corbière, are two bunkers situated at different levels; until the scrap metal merchants got to work in 1953 the upper bunker, a Type 634, mounted a six-loopholed machine-gun turret (*Sechsschartenturm*), while the lower, a Type 633, incorporated a rare *M19* automatic fortress mortar, although the weapon itself was removed by the British Army in 1945.

Fig. 102 - At the foot of the stairs, and in the tunnel looking towards the Type 634 bunker. The standard of construction is high, and here we can see the perfectly formed vaulting. ***Neil Walker***

Fig. 103 - The flights of stairs at the other end of the tunnel leading from the Type 634 bunker. ***Neil Walker***

In 1985 the Channel Islands Occupation Society obtained permission to dig into the buried entrance of the fortress mortar bunker in order to survey the interior. There was considerable surprise on the part of those involved when they found a staircase inside the bunker descending into the depths. From the foot of this staircase a substantial pedestrian tunnel heads off in an easterly direction, at the further end of which is a second staircase, also of considerable length, leading upwards and ending at the foot of an iron runged ladder; this in turn leads into the machine-gun turret bunker at the higher level.

Unusually, there is no defensive machine-gun loophole at either end of this subterranean corridor so that an attacker, having captured one bunker, would have had little difficulty in taking its neighbour. Both bunkers have now been restored by the Society, and are regularly open to the public in the summer months.

Le Mont de la Rocque, St. Brelade

Batterie Derfflinger – A battery of four *8cm FK 30(t)* Czechoslovakian field guns with underground accommodation and support facilities.

By the end of 1941 the 1st and 2nd Battalions of Divisional Artillery Regiment 319 were established in Jersey, with *1./AR 319* (1st Battery) *Derfflinger* installed on the edge of the escarpment overlooking St. Aubin's Harbour.

After the adjacent French coast fell into Allied hands in 1944, there was a shift in defensive effort to the east of the Island (see '*Batterie Schlieffen*' below), and in August of that year, *Derfflinger* was reduced to a *Kanonen Zug* (Gun Platoon). Two of its guns were transferred to the Infantry, and it was thereafter manned by a scratch crew comprised mainly of Headquarters Staff, with the *1./AR 319* personnel moving to *Batterie Fritsch* in St. Lawrence as part of a general reshuffle.

The gunners' quarters, battery HQ, and forward observation post are all connected by underground passageways constructed on the 'cut-and-cover' system by an Army Construction Battalion; thus they are not true tunnels but are of sufficient interest for them to be included in this publication.

Built almost entirely of brick, these passageways

Figs. 104 & 105 - The passageways at *Batterie Derfflinger*. Although mainly brick, some are concrete-lined. *Steve Powell*

Fig. 106 - *Batterie Derfflinger's* forward observation post. *Steve Powell*

Fig. 107 - One of the crew rooms leading off the passageways. Note the light well. *Steve Powell*

extend for a considerable distance through fields on private land, and may only be visited with special permission of the owners.

Le Mont du Coin, St. Brelade

Batterie Seydlitz – A battery of four *8cm FK 30(t)* Czechoslovakian field guns with underground accommodation and support facilities.

Seydlitz (2./AR 319), was the only other divisional artillery battery equipped with 8cm field guns, and was *Derfflinger's* 'nearest neighbour', being established on the edge of the escarpment overlooking La Haule, to the north of St. Aubin, in early 1942 (for a detailed account, see *Channel Islands Occupation Review No.39*, pp.7 -25).

The gun positions and support structures were

Figs. 108 & 109 - *Batterie Seydlitz*: the observation post and adjacent passageways. *Colin Isherwood*

Figs. 110 & 111 - Cristin Bouchet examines some of the more cramped and rudimentary sections of passageway at *Seydlitz*. *Neil Walker*

Fig. 112 - The surviving 8cm field gun emplacement at *Batterie Seydlitz. Colin Isherwood*

inter-connected by underground concrete-lined passageways. Although much of the battery disappeared when the site was developed in the 1960s, large parts of the passageway network survive, together with one of the gun emplacements, the battery HQ, observation post and various shelters.

The passageways were again built on the 'cut-and-cover' system; some are of a field reinforced standard, and others are extremely rudimentary, but all are of sufficient interest and rarity to justify their inclusion in this publication.

As in the case of *Derfflinger*, the remaining structures are on private land, and may only be visited with permission of the owners.

Les Landes Common, St. Ouen

Batterie Moltke – Coastal artillery battery at the north-west corner of the Island.

By the end of 1941, Army Coastal Battery 356 (*HKB 356*) was installed on Les Landes

Fig. 113 - *Batterie Moltke*: part of the extensive subterranean complex serving the 15.5cm gun emplacements.

Fig. 114 - One of the 'cut-and-cover' corridors leading to the ammunition bunkers.
Jeremy Hamon

Common; armed with four *15,5cm K 418(f)* captured French field guns of World War I vintage, the task of the battery was to protect the sea passage between Jersey and Guernsey.

The old French guns were mounted in what were intended to be temporary emplacements as it was the intention that they would be replaced by modern turret-mounted, quick-firing *15cm SK C/28* ship's guns of German manufacture emplaced in gun pits. While awaiting the arrival of these guns, work on the construction of the gun pits and the supporting personnel and ammunition bunkers was pressed energetically ahead, each gun having one of each, with the exception of the No. 4 gun which had two ammunition bunkers.

All these buildings were placed below ground using, once again, the 'cut-and-cover' method of construction which may be seen in RAF aerial reconnaissance photos taken in April, 1943.

The battery was re-constituted as the 5th Battery of Army Coastal Regiment 1265 *(5./HKAR 1265)* in April, 1943, and shortly afterwards it was made known that the modern guns could not be delivered due to the production lines in Germany having been destroyed in air raids. Therefore, the old French guns had to become the permanent armament with their emplacements linked into the subterranean burrowings; the latter, as a visit to *Batterie Moltke* will reveal, contain some fairly lengthy connecting corridors which, despite the fact that they are really nothing more than trenches lined and roofed with reinforced concrete, are sufficiently impressive to be included in this book as tunnels.

The No. 4 gun emplacement was placed in the care of the Channel Islands Occupation Society in 1978 for restoration and conservation purposes. A dedicated team of Society members has restored much of the complex to its original condition. The bunker interiors have been renovated, bunk beds re-fitted and ventilation pumps re-installed, whilst externally, the gun pits have been cleared, and an original gun barrel and carriage reinstated.

Fig. 115 - In the care of the CIOS since 1978, this 'temporary' emplacement for one of the battery's elderly *15,5cm K 418(f)* French field guns was linked to the subterranean ammunition and personnel bunkers by means of an improvised ramp. On display is an original *Moltke* gun, which was dumped over the nearby cliffs by the British Army in 1946, and recovered in 1991.
Jeremy Hamon

Fig. 116 - The adjacent emplacement intended for a modern, turret-mounted *15cm SK C/28* ship's gun, with ammunition hoists linked to the storage complex below. The ship's guns were never installed, and thus the 15.5cm French field guns became the battery's permanent armament. On display are the barrels of a *21cm Mrs 18* howitzer and a *22cm K 532(f)* field gun, used elsewhere in the Island, and recovered from the cliffs in 1993.
Jeremy Hamon

Verclut, Grouville

Batterie Schlieffen – A coastal artillery battery of four *15cm K 18* guns established in September, 1944.

The area known as Verclut, Grouville, stands on high ground in that parish immediately above Fauvic Cross Roads and is not to be confused with Verclut Point at St. Martin. With sweeping views over the entire south-east corner of the Island from Mont Orgueil in the east to Le Hocq in the west, it is hardly surprising that the Germans established Resistance Nest *Verclut* at this point in 1941. The east coast of Jersey remained comparatively lightly defended for most of the Occupation as Hitler's strategic thinking always envisaged a British attack on the Island coming from the west as, according to him, the adjacent French coast would always be in German hands. When the unthinkable happened in July/August, 1944, and the French coast fell to the Americans, some rapid adjustments had to be made and two 15cm coastal artillery batteries were speedily transferred from Guernsey and emplaced on Jersey's east coast. *Batterie Schlieffen* was the name given to the four guns installed at Verclut as *13./HKAR 1265*.

The battery's officers were billeted in the property known as 'Inisfail' on La Rue des Côtils, Grouville, and ever since c.1950 successive owners of that property have wasted much time seeking a tunnel which was supposed to connect the house to the artillery battery in the fields above.

In their belief that there had been a tunnel linking the two points they were correct, but any hopes of finding the subterranean passage were stillborn, as it was merely a deep trench lined with wood and covered with earth. It was ripped up in 1946 and the wood lining was disposed of at an auction sale conducted by Mr. Harold Benest, who sold off many items of German hardware on behalf of the British military authorities in the immediate post-war period.

Fig. 117 - *Batterie Schlieffen*: in this 1945 view, the two wooden posts mark the entrance to the wood-lined underground passage leading to 'Inisfail', La Rue des Côtils, Grouville.
CIOS Collection

6. Myths, Legends & Reality

As already mentioned in Chapter 1 of this book, the German tunnels in the Channel Islands are the cause of more interest than any other type of fortification. According to popular legend there are dozens of 'secret' tunnels with buried entrances running all over the Islands; and being *German* tunnels, they are all alleged to have had a sinister purpose!

All absolute rubbish, of course, yet firmly believed in by people who ought to know better.

The most sinister purpose, according to popular legend, was that they were intended to house gas chambers to exterminate the entire civilian population. Had the German authorities wished to do this, there would have been no need whatsoever for them to excavate dozens of tunnels for the purpose, because any one of the more efficient concentration camps in Germany could have dealt with every man, woman and child in the Channel Islands in the course of a single day, a fact pointed out by Dr. Charles Cruickshank, author of the official history of the Occupation. (*The German Occupation of the Channel Islands*, Oxford University Press, 1975, Chapter 7).

Next in line comes the 'launching of secret weapons' theory. Various 'experts' have appeared from time to time claiming to have definite proof that flying bombs and rockets were to be launched from the Channel Islands' tunnels against England. Anybody with a modicum of common sense will realise that there were scores of more suitable launching sites on the French, Belgian or Dutch coasts (and much closer to England, too!) without going to all the trouble of conveying valuable missiles to the Channel Islands by sea, where they would be at the mercy of prowling warships of the Royal Navy! For the interested, excellent descriptions of genuine V1 and V2 launching sites in France, etc., may be found in *After the Battle*, issue No. 6.

Every schoolboy knows 'for certain' of German tunnels crammed with 'stuff' waiting to be discovered. When the late Richard Mayne opened his Bunker Museum at St. Peter, he was approached on more than one occasion by youngsters who could show him tunnels containing such items as (i) cases of *MG 34* machine-guns, (ii) Tiger tanks, (iii) a complete railway locomotive, and (iv) a Messerschmitt *Bf 109* fighter still in its packing case! He used to tell them, "Lead me to it, my boy, and I'll give you £500 on the spot!"

Needless to say, all the various items are still awaiting discovery!

Then there are the 'undiscovered' tunnels! In St. Ouen's Bay there are two – one running from the car park of the 'El Tico' café to the site of the former 'Lobster Pot' restaurant at L'Etacq, and another from the foot of Mont à la Brune to Beaumont; in the east of the Island *Ho Mole Verclut* was intended to be the start of an underground railway which would have conveyed wounded troops, brought to St. Catherine's Breakwater by hospital ship from France, all the way to the Underground Hospital at St. Lawrence; beneath Noirmont Point there is a tunnel large enough to take two double decker buses side by side, running from the tip of the headland right back to Warren Farm; there is a large underground cinema at La Moye, and the appearance of two U-boats off the north coast of Jersey in 1943 means that there must be a 'secret' submarine pen somewhere between Bouley Bay and Bonne Nuit Bay. (Sinel's *Diary*, entry for 28.2.43 refers).

All these stories are firmly believed in by the gullible. Perhaps the best illustration of imaginary tunnels came from a gentleman who insisted that, as a small child in the 1960s, he had regularly played in a tunnel which commenced in the front garden of a house called 'The Homestead' in Vallée des Vaux, and ran right through to Grands Vaux, a distance of some three-quarters of a mile; he had regularly traversed the entire length of this tunnel, he claimed. Attempts to tell him otherwise were to no avail. He was adamant, and added that, as the then owner was worried about accidents, he had caused the tunnel roof to be blown in at three different points … "and if you don't believe me, ask him!" We did, and the former owner of

'The Homestead' roared with laughter! The alleged tunnel was nothing more than a subterranean store in an excavated cavern, although, admittedly it looked like a small tunnel entrance from the outside. He was able to relate that when his late father-in-law purchased the property as long ago as 1946, even then there were stories of German weapons concealed behind a false wall at the rear of this shelter; to clear up the matter, the Royal Engineers (who were still working in the Island at the time) were asked to investigate. They did, and after much hammering and probing, were able to report that the rear of the shelter consisted of nothing but solid rock. Despite this, local folklore still insists that there is a concealed tunnel.

It may be said that if every imaginary German tunnel said to exist in Jersey did, in fact, exist, then the Island would fold in upon itself!

Then there is the much visited *Ho 8* (Jersey War Tunnels) which gets the blame for everything. As an example, the following was overheard on the car ferry as it was crossing St. Aubin's Bay ... "and over yonder's the Underground Hospital where the Germans bricked in 2,000 Spaniards and Russians when they had nothing more to feed them with!" The same tunnel also contains a secret hoard of 'Nazi gold' waiting to be found. And, of course, all the walls are filled with Russian bodies which were disposed of in the wet concrete when they died at work.

It is not denied that there are Russians inside *Ho 8*, but these are buried beneath rockfalls, as no engineer would contemplate having decomposing organic matter in the tunnel lining which would be weakened in consequence. There are even elderly Jerseymen who will tell you that they saw the bodies of Russians, who had died at other building sites, being loaded onto lorries to be taken to *Ho 8* to be tipped into the wet concrete. Why it always has to be *Ho 8*, when there were plenty of other tunnels under construction in the Island, is somewhat unclear!

All these myths and legends are the bread and butter of coach drivers whose passengers lap them up; unfortunately they are encouraged by some travel and guide book writers who would do well to check their facts before rushing into print. On the credit side, however, the States of Jersey Tourism Department now runs what are known as Guide Schemes which coach drivers, and anybody else connected with the tourism industry, can attend if they wish to learn the true facts concerning all aspects of Jersey's history.

Ignoring all these fanciful and false theories, it has to be said that the German tunnels in the Channel Islands have attracted a certain aura of mystique, and many people seem to have the impression that they are in some way unique and of such magnitude that nothing else can approach them. Yet how extensive are they in reality?

It is agreed that the construction of the Channel Islands' tunnels was no mean feat, particularly in view of the fact that by 1st February 1944, the amount of spoil extracted by the *OT* in the course of tunnelling totalled no less than 244,000 cubic metres, whereas the entire Atlantic Wall from Norway to the Spanish border, and not counting the Channel Islands, had yielded a mere 255,000m^3. Yet how does this compare with military tunnelling on the British side?

It would appear that, when indulging in tunnelling, the British have always tended to make use of existing facilities in the shape of old mines, or by extending natural caves, as typified in the following four sites:–

i) At Farleigh Rise, Monkton Farleigh, in the county of Wiltshire, an old subterranean quarry, first opened in 1752 for the extraction of Bath Stone, was adapted to become the largest underground ammunition depot in Europe; with war looming, the mines were taken over by the War Office in 1938, when no less than 7,500 labourers were brought in to extend and adapt the mines to house 165,000 tons of high explosive.

Conveyor belts and narrow gauge railways were installed to connect up with the main Great Western Railway line which ran right up to, and inside, the tunnel entrance. The main tunnel was several miles long and the entire complex was lit by 25,000 lights which burned 24 hours a day. In the event of a mains power failure, there was an enormous diesel-driven dynamo housed in a vast cavern; the air conditioning plant alone cost £250,000 and this was in 1943!

The complex was closed down in the late 1970s and, regrettably, heavily vandalised when scrap metal thieves tore out much of the electrical fittings, wiring and ventilation system, and what they could not remove, they smashed. Undeterred, a group of enthusiasts obtained permission to open part of the mines as a tourist attraction – to have attempted to open the entire complex would have cost a small fortune and visitors would have needed lots of stamina to inspect everything.

The museum was a success, but, unfortunately, following a change of ownership, the mines are now closed; this is a minor tragedy as they are unique and a prime example of British tunnelling ingenuity. To illustrate their size, it can be said that all the German tunnels in Jersey could be fitted inside them, still leaving room to spare! (For a full description, see *Underground Britain*, Webb & Bower, 1988, p.74).

ii) Worthy of mention is 21 Maintenance Unit, RAF, based at Fauld, Staffordshire. In 1937 the Air Ministry took over some abandoned gypsum mines beneath the Stonepit Hills. Extended in 1941, these tunnels eventually housed 20,000 tons of high explosive and incendiary bombs in chambers created by the original mining, these being lined with concrete 2ft. 6ins. thick, and further strengthened by the addition of blast walls.

On 27th November 1944, and for reasons unknown, there was an explosion inside the complex which, in turn, detonated 3,500 tons of high explosive bombs en masse. No less than 68 people were killed, an entire farm and its occupants vanished, and the resulting crater was 80 feet deep and covered an area of 12 acres. (See *After the Battle*, issue No. 18)

iii) Lying 200 feet beneath a sandstone hill at Wolverley, near Kidderminster in the county of Worcestershire, are tunnels covering an area of some 250,000 square feet. The grid pattern galleries range in width from between five and thirty feet and were used as factory workshops during World War II. Two-thirds of the complex were mothballed after the war, but the remainder was fitted out with a canteen, dormitories, generators, water supplies, a sewerage system and an air conditioned temperature of 69°F, all to be used as an emergency administration centre in the event of a nuclear attack. (See *The Sunday Telegraph* for 8.8.93).

iv) Finally, in Gibraltar, which is roughly the size of Alderney, there are no less than 34 miles of tunnels; these were commenced in the 18th Century by Sergeant Major Ince of the Corps of Sappers, and completed in 1968 by their successors, the Royal Engineers. The greatest expansion took place during the Second World War when RE Mining Companies were formed, mainly from coal miners and soft-rock miners, aided by a Canadian tunnelling company. The spoil extracted was used to extend the main airport runway out to sea which, of course, is still used today.

The tunnels occur on several levels and contain headquarters facilities, storage chambers, generators, accommodation for 15,001 personnel, two underground hospitals, and a motor vehicle repair workshop. All the German tunnels in the Channel Islands could be fitted inside this vast subterranean system and, again, there would still be room to spare. A very detailed description of Gibraltar's tunnels is given in *After the Battle*, issue No. 21.

These are but four examples of British military tunnelling and there are many, many more besides, such as the tunnels beneath Dover Castle and some twelve miles of defensive tunnels beneath London, although their full extent has never been fully revealed. (See *Tunnels under London* by Nigel Pennick, The Electric Traction

Society, 1981; and *London under London* by Richard Trench and Ellis Hillman, John Murray, 1984, and re-printed in 1993).

Alongside these enormous subterranean burrowings, the German tunnels in the Channel Islands pale into insignificance as mere scratchings in the ground, and make one realise that in the final analysis, when it comes to tunnelling, and with their long association with mining in all its forms, the British are second to none!

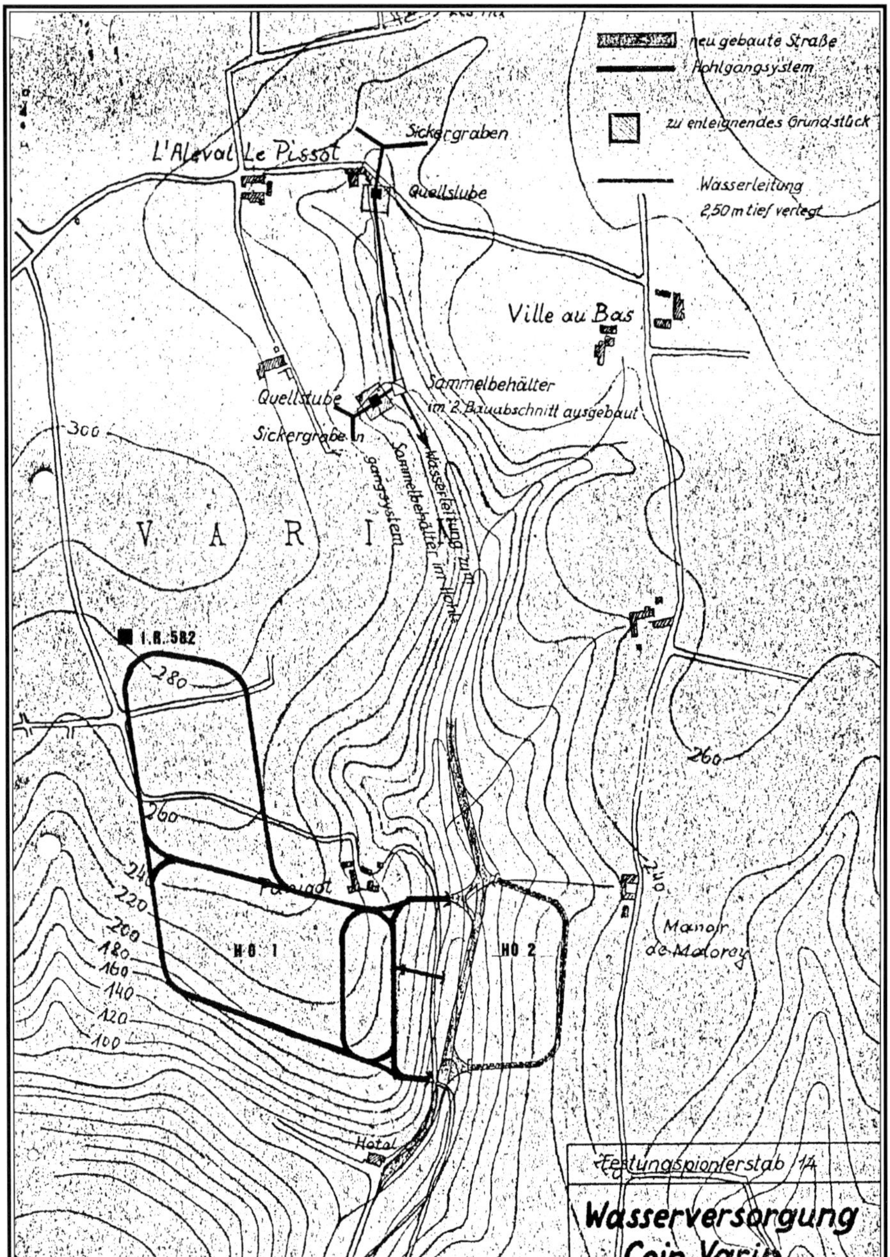

Fig. 118 - Original German map which shows, amongst other things, the planned extent of *Ho 1* in 1942.

Appendix I – The Enigma of *Ho 1*

It was axiomatic that all accommodation tunnels for reserve troops should have an adequate supply of water, and so it comes as no surprise to learn that *Ho 8* was provided with its own well which could (and still does!), supply copious quantities of this commodity.

The recent discovery of an original German map, however, reveals that it was the intention of *Festpistab 14*, in Jersey, to supply the storage tunnels *Ho 1* and *Ho 2*, in what is now La Route de l'Aleval, with fresh water gathered from springs higher up the valley at Le Pissot. On 18th August 1942 a letter was sent to the *Feldkommandantur* requesting them to requisition the necessary land so that two *Quellstuben* (literally, 'spring' or 'well chambers'), could be constructed, one in the yard of the house known as 'Le Pissot', and the other 250 yards lower down the valley towards the tunnels – see the map opposite.

Both still survive, although the second can only be reached by penetrating dense scrub and bushes. It was the construction work associated with the latter *Quellstube* that led to the erroneous belief that the tunnel *Ho 6* was sited here.

These chambers were to be supplied by two *Sickergraben*, or drainage channels; over the gate of the field opposite 'Le Pissot' can still be seen the concrete-work of the *Sickergrabe* for the *Quellstube* in the garden of the house; both are still in operation.

For the benefit of the curious, translations of the other German phrases on the map are as follows:–

Sammelbehälter im 2.Bauabschnitt ausgebaut = Collection reservoir will be constructed in the Second Construction Programme.

Wasserleitung zum Sammelbehälter im Hohlgangsystem = Water main to collection reservoir in the tunnel systems.

neu gebaute Straße = Newly built road.

zu enteignendes Grundstück = Requisitioned premises.

Wasserleitung 2,50m tief verlegt = Water main laid 2.50 metres deep.

However, the most interesting thing about the map is that it clearly shows how the two tunnel systems *Ho 1* and *Ho 2* were intended to be when first planned in 1941. It will be seen that *Ho 2* was intended to be a simple loop but, on the other hand, *Ho 1* was to have been of considerable size, stretching right back beneath the area of Le Panigot and almost as far as the Regimental Commander's HQ bunker at Battle Headquarters at Coin Varin. The only alterations that we have made to the original map are to enhance the tracing of *Ho 1*; to add the tunnel numbers; and to mark the position of the Command Bunker opposite 'The White House'.

Now study Figs. 120 and 121 ... the former is a schematic diagram copied from the 1942 map to show what was planned at that time; the latter shows what had happened by 1945 and what *might* lie behind two roof-falls. The unlined sections of *Ho 1* are remarkable in that they contain only one or two very minor rockfalls; yet lurking at the rear of the uncompleted northern section of the complex are two headings which are completely blocked by major roof-falls.

Let us now refer to the personal photograph album-cum-diary of Major F. Sargent, RAOC, (now held in the Jersey Archive) the contents of which were reproduced in the *Jersey Evening Post*, issues for 20th August 1992, *et seq.*, and particularly that for 25th August. Referring to the disposal of German artillery pieces in 1946, the Major wrote "... the next method of disposal was to stuff the smaller guns into part of the St. Peter's Valley tunnel and then blow the end in. I imagine that they will not be very good in a year or two. We got rid of quite a few 47, 75 and 105-millimetre weapons in other parts of the tunnels. Altogether we got rid of over 200 guns in this manner."

The fact that the blown in galleries of *Ho 2* over the road contain German guns is known, but now *Ho 1* comes into the picture. Now study Fig.121

Fig. 119 - Major Sargent, RAOC, stands alongside some 2cm anti-aircraft guns which are about to be immurred behind concrete block walls in *Ho 1*, in February, 1946. Unlike those buried behind roof-falls, they were smartly extracted when the scrap metal drive commenced in 1953. *Jersey Evening Post*

again ... because of poor lighting and the fact that the associated headings were always filled with thigh-deep pools of water held in check by low block walls, it had always been assumed that the rock-falls shown at A and C in the diagram were dead ends. However, with the intelligence revealed in Major Sargent's diary, we decided to investigate and sought permission from Jersey Mushroom Growers so to do; this was duly given but with a warning that the investigations would have to be done within seven days as, due to the presence of spores which were detrimental to the cultivation of mushrooms present in the relevant galleries, the ends were to be firmly sealed.

Paul Burnal was volunteered to plumb the depths of the 50-yard long pools of evil-looking water, and duly returned to report that the far ends of the galleries did not terminate in dead-ends but in roof-falls ... Major Sargent's roof-falls, no doubt! The question is – how far do the galleries proceed beyond the roof-falls?

It can be taken that the heading X-Y-Z on the diagram does not exist as there is a dead end at X, but what about A-B-C? How far do the galleries go? Does the entire loop exist, filled with dismantled German weapons? We will never know the answer.

Ho 1
1942

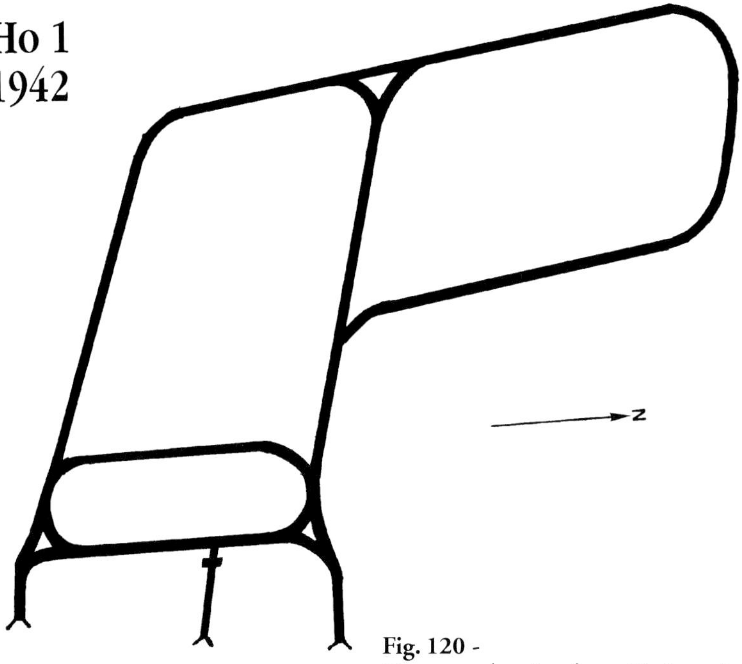

Fig. 120 -
Diagram showing how *Ho 1* was intended to be in 1942.

Ho 1
1945

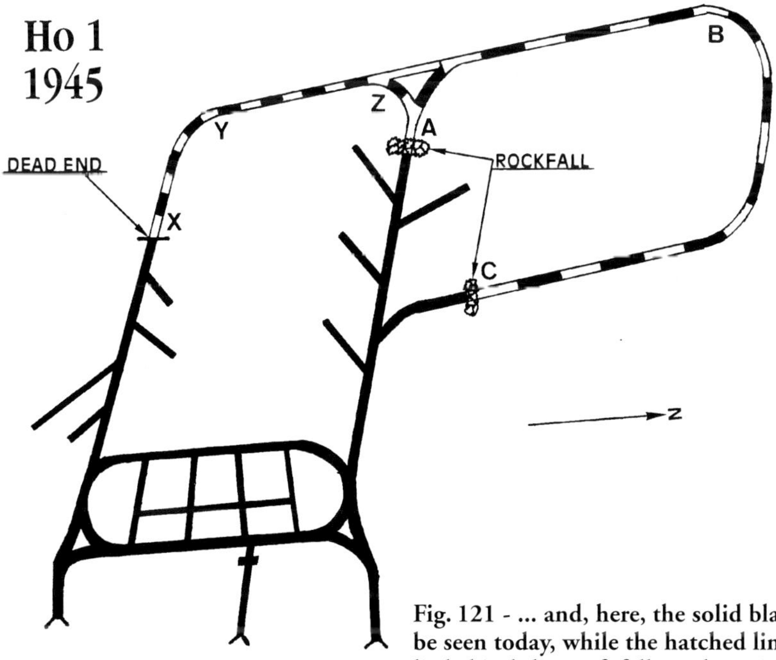

Fig. 121 - ... and, here, the solid black lines show what can be seen today, while the hatched lines indicate what MAY lie behind the roof-falls at the points marked A and C.

WANTON DAMAGE

THE officer in charge and the members of the Forces engaged in rehabilitation work at the former German Hospital in St. Peter's Valley are much concerned over the senseless and wanton acts of damage perpetrated by some individual or individuals, acts which hold up the work and cause considerable annoyance and inconvenience to all concerned

The entrance to the hospital was guarded by a heavy door with a very large padlock but this was forced by crowbars and someone obtained admittance and stole the fuel injector of the Diesel engine. This engine runs the lighting plant which was specially designed for the job, and the fuel injector, which was removed by means of spanners and screwdrivers, is of no use to anyone at all. Now the whole plant has been put out of action and considerable expense is involved, for the military, who were using this lighting system, will now have to come on to the public supply, which will necessitate the laying of mains or they will have to install another engine.

A squad of men has been engaged for the last two days trying to get the plant going but are unable to do so, and all work in the tunnel is now at a standstill.

Some irresponsible persons have also entered the ammunition tunnel at various times, and we are asked to remind folk that there is absolutely nothing of interest to be seen either in the tunnel or in the hospital, so please keep out.

We appeal to the thieves to restore the machine parts which they have taken.

31st January 1946

DUMP RUBBISH IN TUNNELS

Dear Sir,—I read with pleasure your admirable account of the military "tidying-up" operations in the Island, and would suggest that before the tunnels and pits are finally "sealed up" could they not be persuaded to hold many, if not all, of the derelict cars and other unsightly "dumping ground" furniture? It is a sorry sight to see so much of our beautiful valleys and cliffs strewn with such ugly and unwholesome rubbish.

I am,

Yours truly,

"A LOVER OF JERSEY."

28th February 1946

Occupation 'Show-Places'

WHEN we reported the celebrations attending the first anniversary of Jersey's liberation, we mentioned that hundreds of folk during the afternoon paid a visit to the German underground hospital and tunnels in St. Peter's Valley. There is no doubt that very many more local folk will want to visit these legacies of the German occupation and it is not difficult to realize the "appeal" they will make to visitors to the Island. With this in mind, we suggest that arrangements should be made to open both the "hospital" and the tunnel to the public on Thursday and Sunday afternoons. Should the argument be advanced that this would necessitate keeping someone on duty at each of these places on these particular days, we feel that this could quite easily be met by making an admission charge of one shilling, which would more than cover whatever expense was involved. If the authorities concerned, whether military or civil, have no wish to profit from such an arrangement as we suggest, we have no doubt that the Jersey branch of the British Legion, or some similar ex-Service organization, would willingly accept any credit balance which might accrue. There must be thousands of local folk who have not seen, but would like to see what are now undoubted "show places," and the fact that the owners of motor coaches already include these places in their itinerary is an indication of the attraction they would have to visitors, particularly if explanatory notices were set up in the various sections. At any rate we make the suggestion in the hope that it will be considered by the authorities.

21st May 1946

Appendix II – Tunnel Statistics

The following statistics appertaining to the excavation of the Channel Islands' tunnels have been gathered from the monthly Fortress Engineers Building Progress Reports.

The first part relates to the amount of square meterage of floor space under construction and completed month by month. Unfortunately, not all the Reports have survived.

Key:- a) = Under construction b) = Progress during the past month c) = Completed

			GUERNSEY	**JERSEY**	**ALDERNEY**
Total amount of storage floor space planned for each Island:–					
(All figures in square metres)			**22,000**	**18,000**	**10,000**
1942		a)	1,350	2,400	250
	APRIL	b)	Not shown	Not shown	Not shown
		c)	Nil	Nil	Nil
		a)	9,230	7,890	250
	OCTOBER	b)	Not shown	Not shown	Not shown
		c)	Nil	Nil	Nil
1943		a)	16,278	18,801(1)	2,882
	APRIL	b)	1,210	2,560	629
		c)	Nil	Nil	Nil
		a)	18,645	20,925	3,353
	MAY	b)	2,367	1,724	471
		c)	Nil	Nil	Nil
		a)	17,641	16,184	3,896
	JUNE	b)	See note (2)	981 (3)	543
		c)	Nil	Nil	Nil
		a)	18,581	20,043	4,211
	JULY	b)	940	3,859	315
		c)	597	2,552	Nil
		a)	19,447	22,582	4,516
	AUGUST	b)	866	2,539	305
		c)	597	2,839	Nil
		a)	20,187	23,054	4,795
	SEPTEMBER	b)	740	472	279
		c)	597	2,552	Nil

No reports were submitted for October and November, 1943, due to the run-down of the Fortress Engineers and the *OT* who were being returned to the Continent.

	a)	20,233	24,600	4,795
DECEMBER	b)	Nil	186	Nil
	c)	1,097	2,794	Nil

Appendix II / continued ...

1944		a)	20,338	24,089 (4)	4,795
	JANUARY	b)	105	Nil	Nil
		c)	1,097	2,794	Nil
		a)	20,338	24,089	4,795
	FEBRUARY	b)	Nil	Nil	Nil
		c)	1,097	2,794	Nil
		a)	19,166 (4)	23,495 (4)	4,795
	MARCH	b)	140	Nil	Nil
		c)	1,097	2,794	Nil
		a)	19,216	23,495	4,795
	APRIL	b)	50	Nil	Nil
		c)	1,097	2,794	Nil

At this point the Fortress Engineer reports cease due to D-Day.

Notes:-

1) Reason for exceeding the planned total is due to the standardisation of the profile of cross-galleries.

2) The *OT* has reported the total for *Ho 40* twice; an amendment will be made.

3) The *OT* has reported 5,322m^2 too much; a correction will be made.

4) The total amount reduced on the basis of local verification.

The following figures give the total amount of rock extracted during the course of tunnelling on all three Islands during 1943 and up to April, 1944. (All figures in cubic metres):–

1943	**March** :	13,500	
	April :	16,271	
	May :	25,230	
	June :	11,382	(Army Rock Drilling Companies despatched to the South of France)
	July :	14,291	
	August :	15,088	
	September :	14,218	
	October :	10,323	
	November :	6,736	(Strength of *OT* being greatly reduced)
	December :	3,258	
1944	**January** :	1,296	(Strength of *OT* still further reduced)
	February :	1,043	
	March :	3,370	
	April :	837	(Actual tunnelling almost at a standstill; workforce concentrated on consolidating tunnel interiors)

By January, 1944, 244,000m^3 of rock have been extracted; the entire Atlantic Wall, from Norway to the Spanish border - not counting the Channel Islands - has yielded 255,000m^3.

Appendix III - Tunnel Plans

The plans of *Ho 1, 2, 4, 10, 13* and *15* are based on those prepared by the British Army in 1962. Although helpful, the plans had to be checked out on the ground wherever possible as they had not been correctly drawn up in the first place. As stated in Chapter 1, all curves had been eliminated and substituted by a series of sharp angles; this was probably done at the time for speed of compilation, but the result was far from satisfactory. For the set of plans that appeared in *German Tunnels in the Channel Islands*, Paul Burnal re-reinstated the curves, corrected errors, and added information; and for this present publication, the plans were reviewed and further enhanced with the use of computer graphics. However, it should be emphasised that whilst the aim is to provide a reasonably accurate guide to the basic layout and design of each complex, the plans are not intended to be technically precise.

The then States of Jersey Public Services Department (now TTS) provided the plan of *Ho 5*, while the plan of *Ho 8* (taken from a c.1948 guide book) has been reproduced by kind permission of the Jersey War Tunnels. For this publication, Stewart Logan of the TTS kindly provided an updated, digitally-mapped plan of *Ho 19/20*, while Neil Walker provided the new plan of *Batterie Seydlitz*. The plans for *Ho Etacquerel* and *Ho Mole Verclut*, as well as those for batteries *Derfflinger* and *Moltke*, and strongpoints *Corbiere* and *Doktorhaus*, had to be surveyed from scratch and, apart from some minor amendments and graphic enhancement, are much as they appeared in *German Tunnels in the Channel Islands*.

It would be nice to think that one day some original *Festpistab* plans of the Channel Islands' tunnels will be found. Extensive enquiries in various archive sources have so far proved negative but - who knows - perhaps one day they will be discovered, gathering dust at the back of some shelf, having been wrongly filed at some time in the distant past!

Fig. 122 - Paul Burnal double-checking measurements at *Ho 1* in 2012. *Matthew Costard*

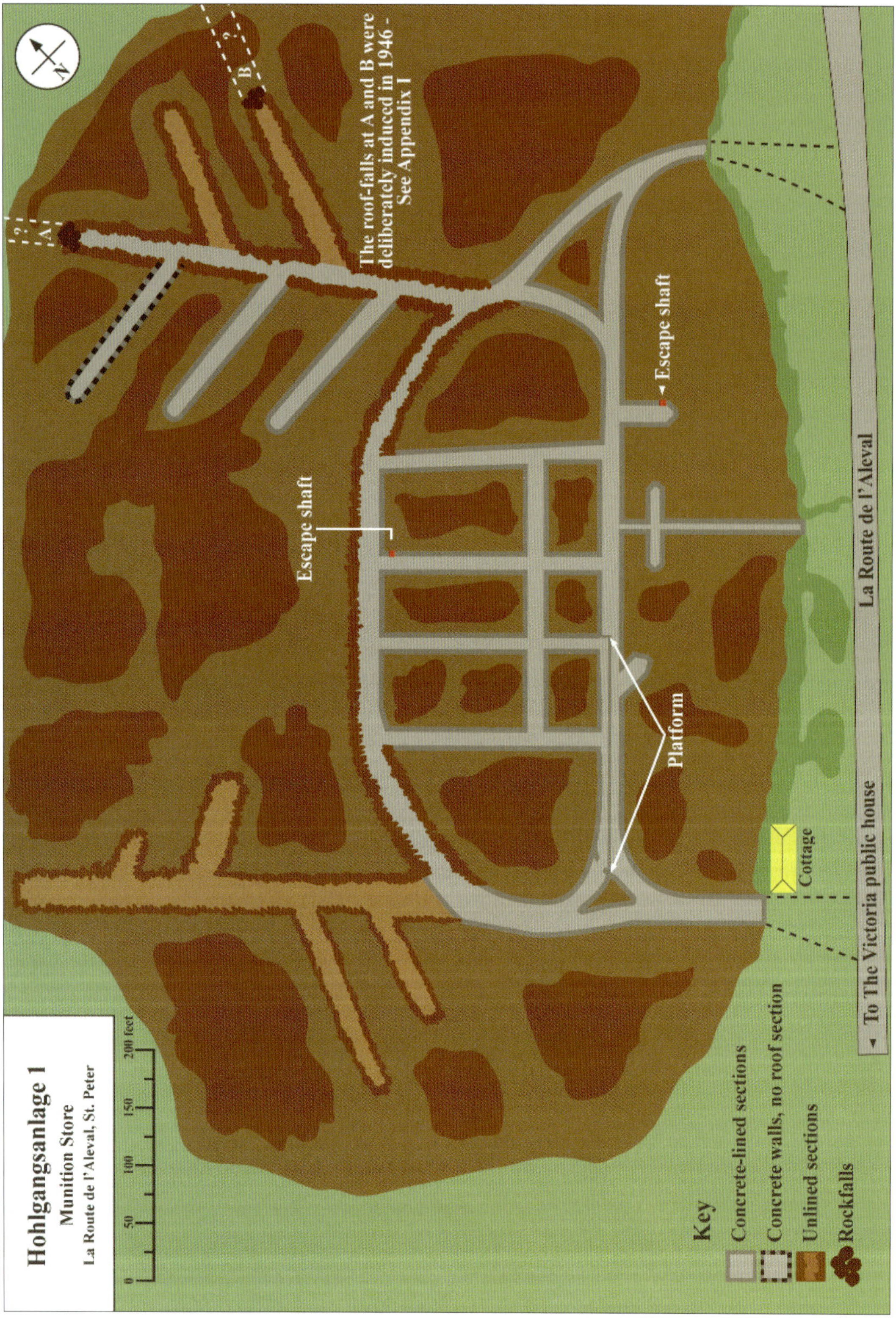

Hohlgangsanlage 1
Munition Store
La Route de l'Aleval, St. Peter
0
50
100
150
200 feet
Key
Concrete-lined sections
Concrete walls, no roof section
Unlined sections
Rockfalls
N
A
B
?
?
The roof-falls at A and B were deliberately induced in 1946 - See Appendix I
Escape shaft
Escape shaft
Platform
Cottage
La Route de l'Aleval
To The Victoria public house

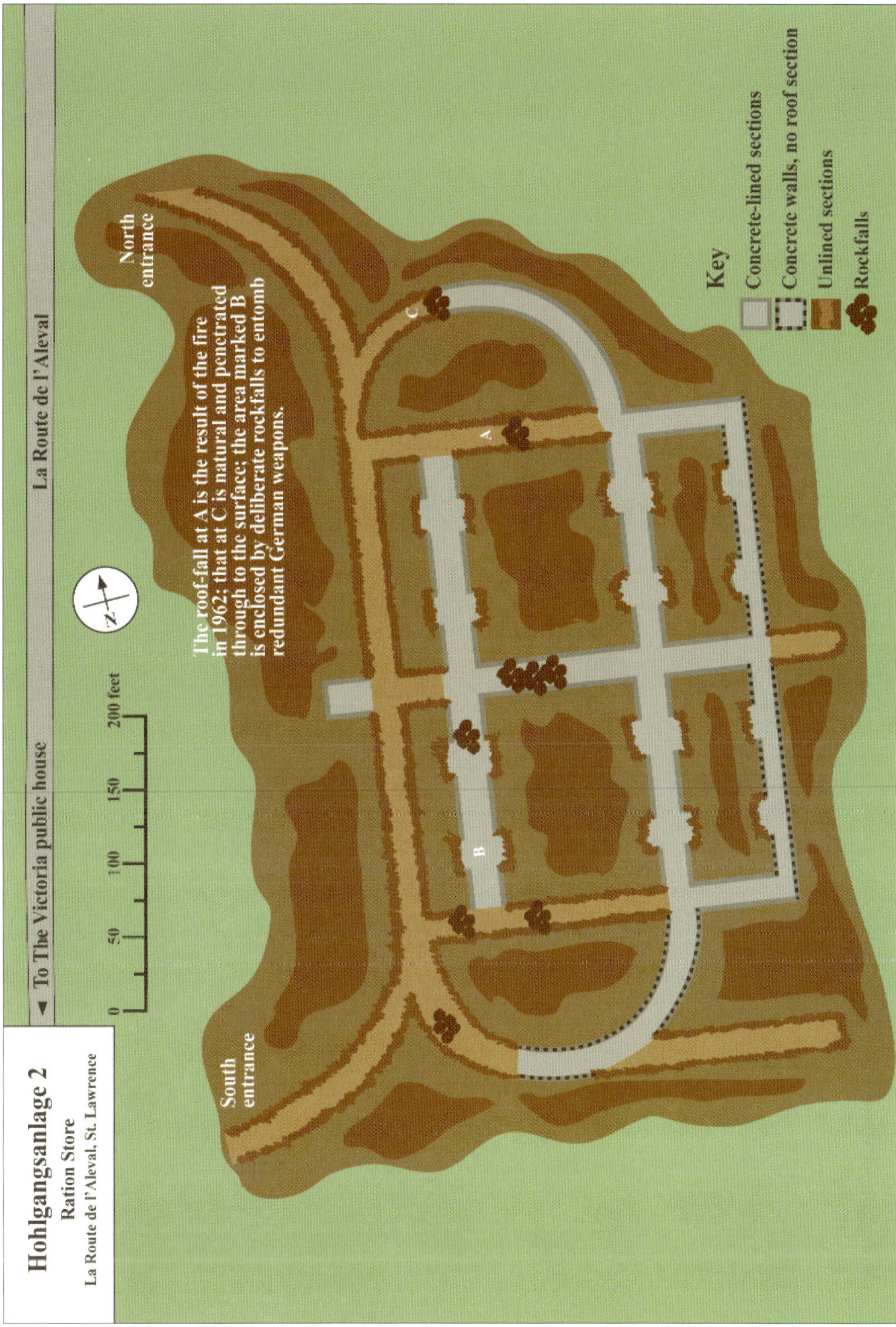
Hohlgangsanlage 2
Ration Store
La Route de l'Aleval, St. Lawrence
◄ To The Victoria public house
La Route de l'Aleval
0 50 100 150 200 feet
N
South entrance
North entrance
A
B
C
The roof-fall at A is the result of the fire in 1962; that at C is natural and penetrated through to the surface; the area marked B is enclosed by deliberate rockfalls to entomb redundant German weapons.
Key
Concrete-lined sections
Concrete walls, no roof section
Unlined sections
Rockfalls

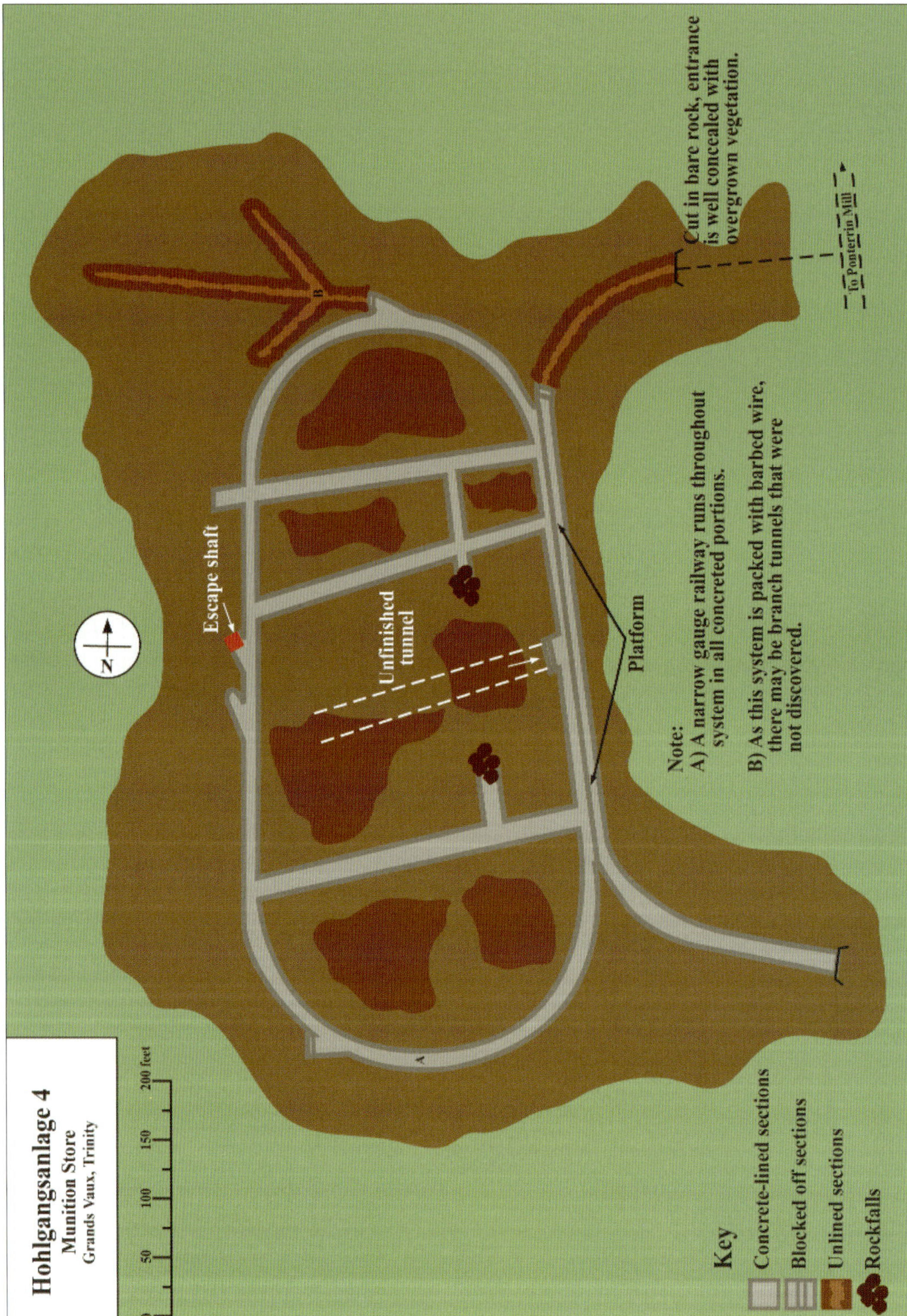

Hohlgangsanlage 4
Munition Store
Grands Vaux, Trinity
0 50 100 150 200 feet
Key
Concrete-lined sections
Blocked off sections
Unlined sections
Rockfalls
Escape shaft
Unfinished tunnel
Platform
Note:
A) A narrow gauge railway runs throughout system in all concreted portions.
B) As this system is packed with barbed wire, there may be branch tunnels that were not discovered.
Cut in bare rock, entrance is well concealed with overgrown vegetation.
To Ponterrin Mill
N
A
B

Hohlgangsanlage 5
Fuel Store (in practice, used as Munition Store)
Railway Walk, St. Aubin
0 10 M
All tunnels are lined
Escape shaft
UP
Former Jersey Railways tunnel
Railway track to La Corbière
St. Aubin

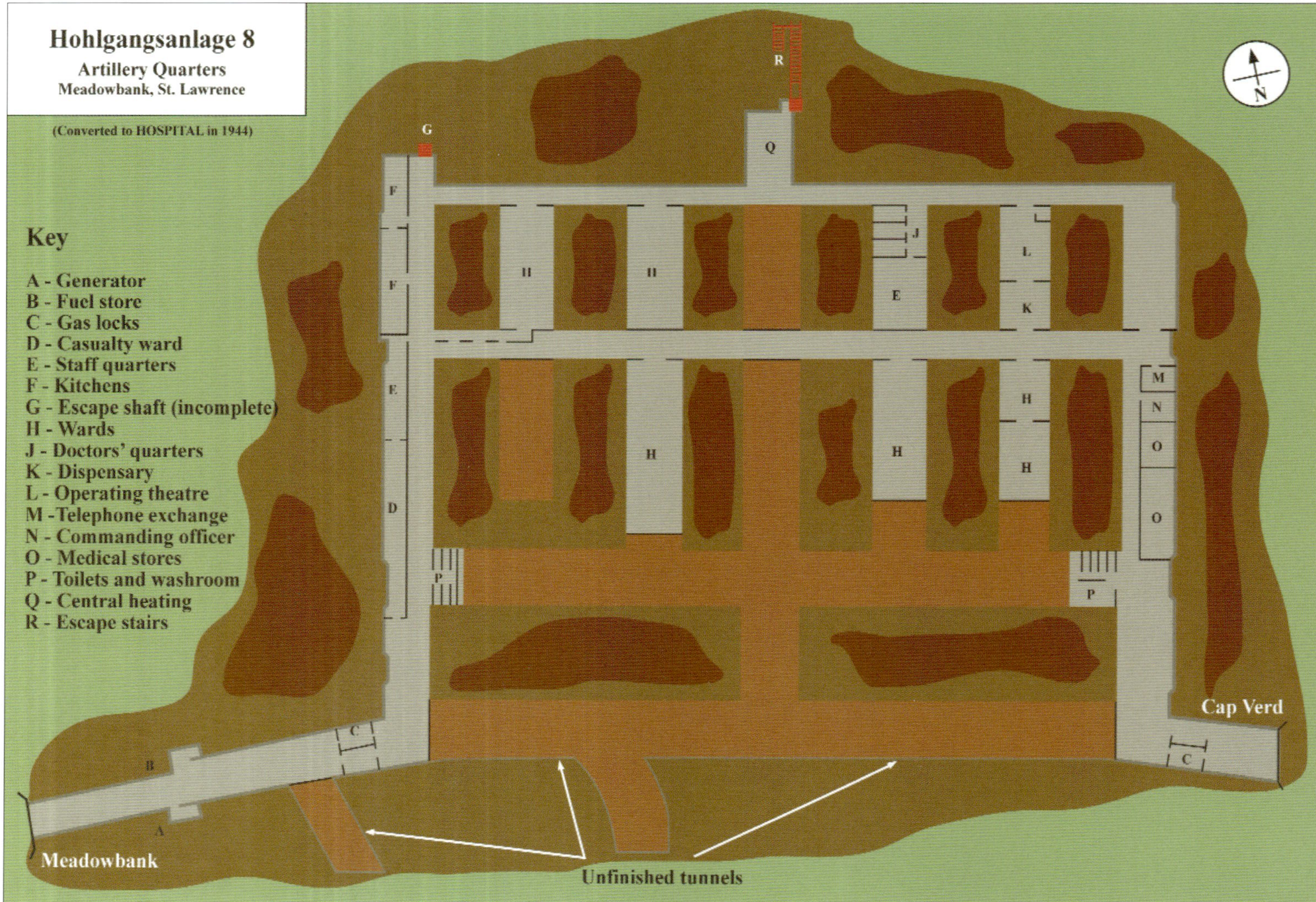
Hohlgangsanlage 8
Artillery Quarters
Meadowbank, St. Lawrence
(Converted to HOSPITAL in 1944)
Key
A - Generator
B - Fuel store
C - Gas locks
D - Casualty ward
E - Staff quarters
F - Kitchens
G - Escape shaft (incomplete)
H - Wards
J - Doctors' quarters
K - Dispensary
L - Operating theatre
M -Telephone exchange
N - Commanding officer
O - Medical stores
P - Toilets and washroom
Q - Central heating
R - Escape stairs
Meadowbank
Cap Verd
Unfinished tunnels
N

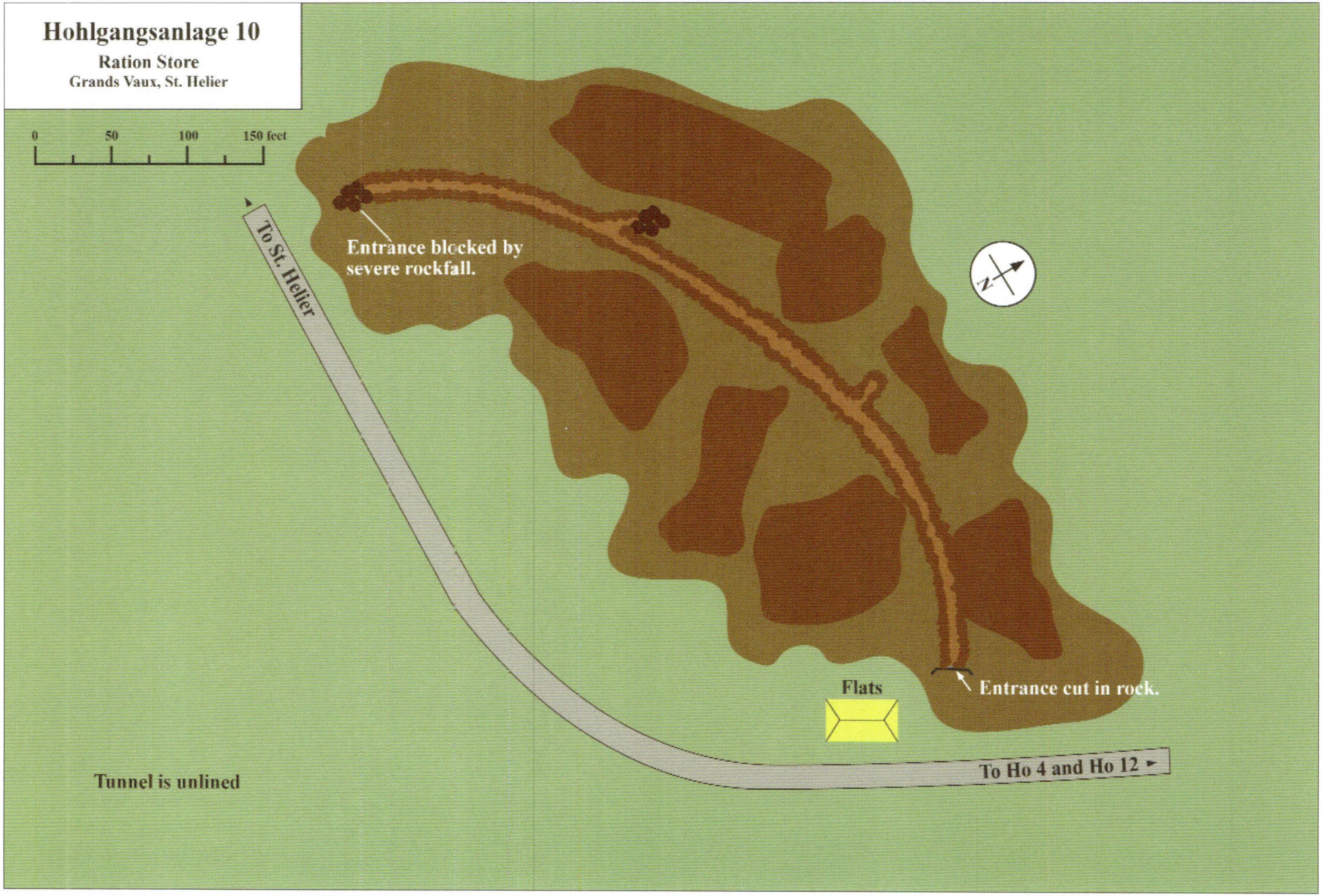

Hohlgangsanlage 10
Ration Store
Grands Vaux, St. Helier
0
50
100
150 feet
Entrance blocked by severe rockfall.
To St. Helier
Flats
Entrance cut in rock.
To Ho 4 and Ho 12
Tunnel is unlined

Hohlgangsanlage 13
Munition Store (unused)
Beaumont Valley, St. Peter
0
50
100
150
200 feet
N
Escape shaft
Cross-hatched portion of tunnel
was too dangerous to survey.
Garage
To Beaumont Hill
Track to Ho 15
Key
Concrete-lined section (walls only)
Unlined sections

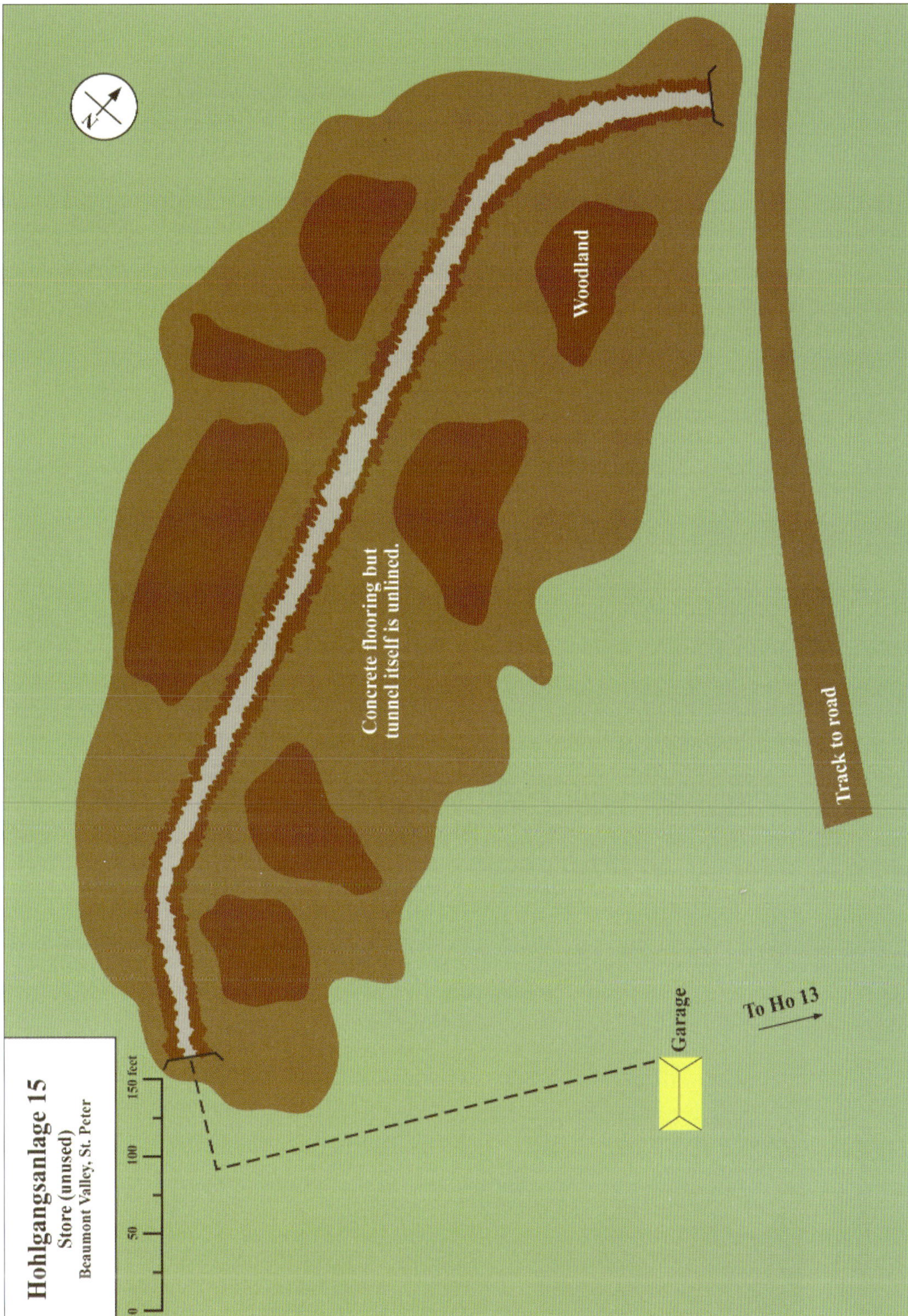
Hohlgangsanlage 15
Store (unused)
Beaumont Valley, St. Peter
0
50
100
150 feet
N
Woodland
Concrete flooring but tunnel itself is unlined.
Track to road
Garage
To Ho 13

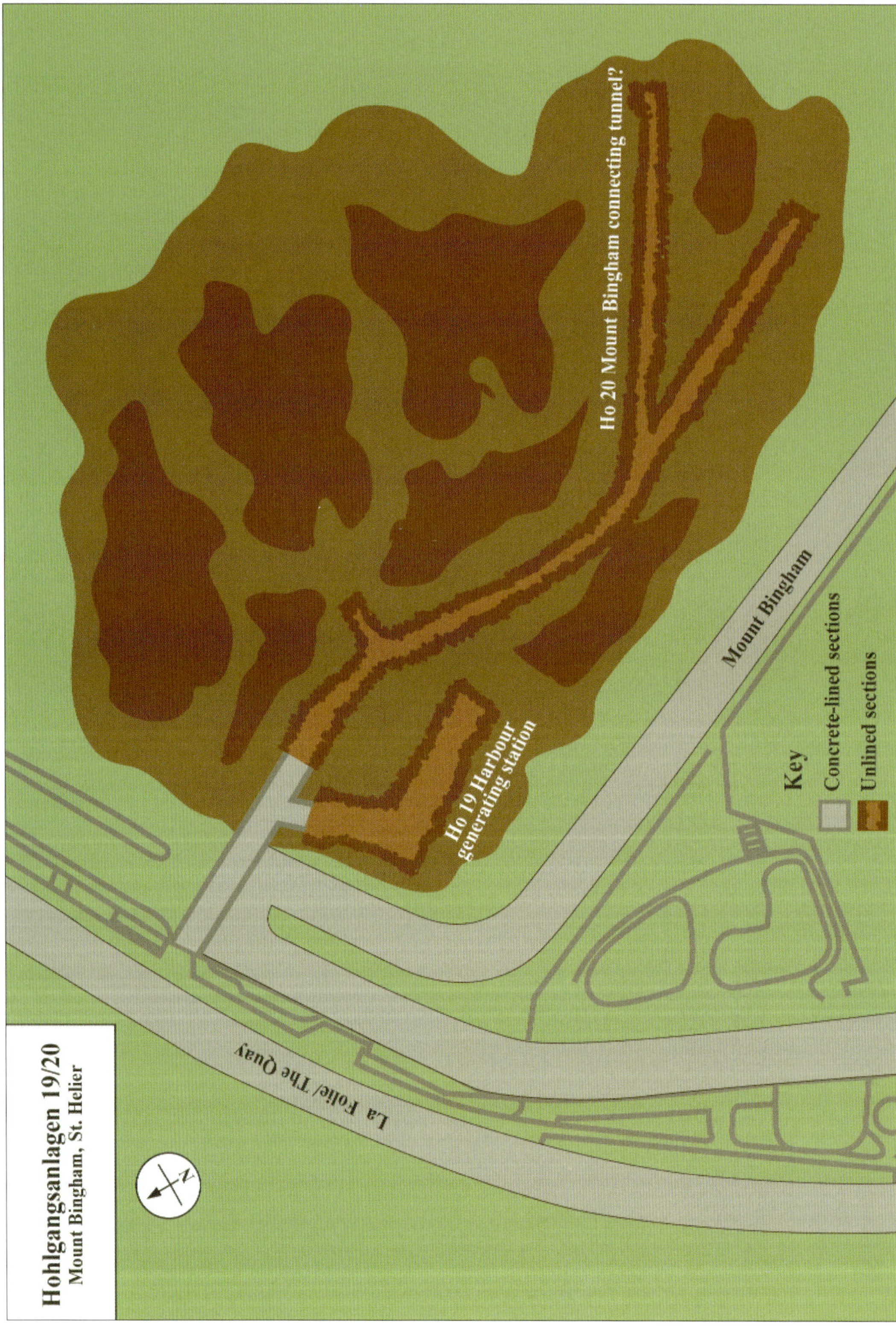
Hohlgangsanlagen 19/20
Mount Bingham, St. Helier
N
Ho 20 Mount Bingham connecting tunnel?
Ho 19 Harbour generating station
Mount Bingham
La Folie/ The Quay
Key
Concrete-lined sections
Unlined sections

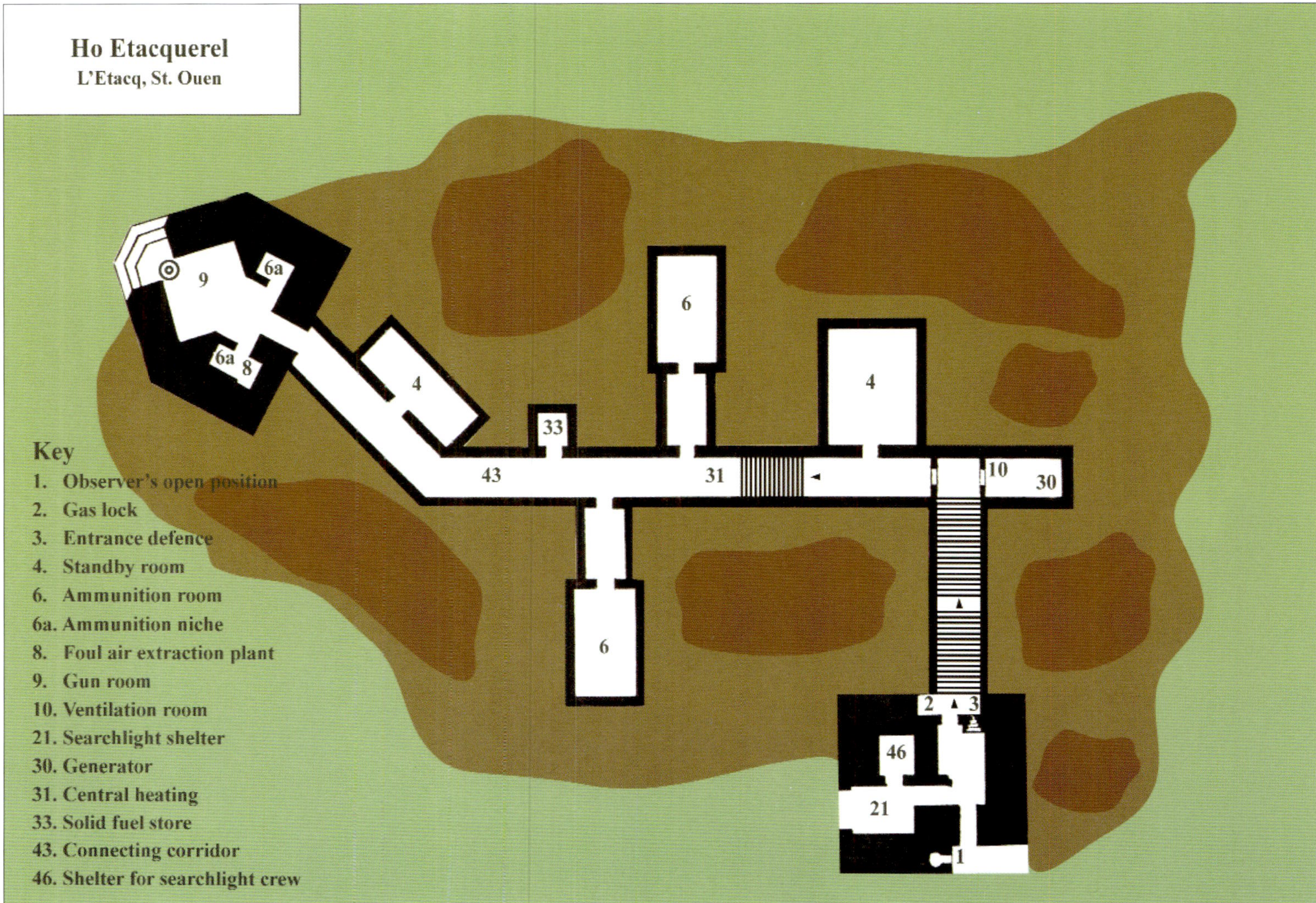
Ho Etacquerel
L'Etacq, St. Ouen
Key
1. Observer's open position
2. Gas lock
3. Entrance defence
4. Standby room
6. Ammunition room
6a. Ammunition niche
8. Foul air extraction plant
9. Gun room
10. Ventilation room
21. Searchlight shelter
30. Generator
31. Central heating
33. Solid fuel store
43. Connecting corridor
46. Shelter for searchlight crew
9
6a
6a
8
4
33
6
4
43
31
10
30
6
2
3
46
21
1

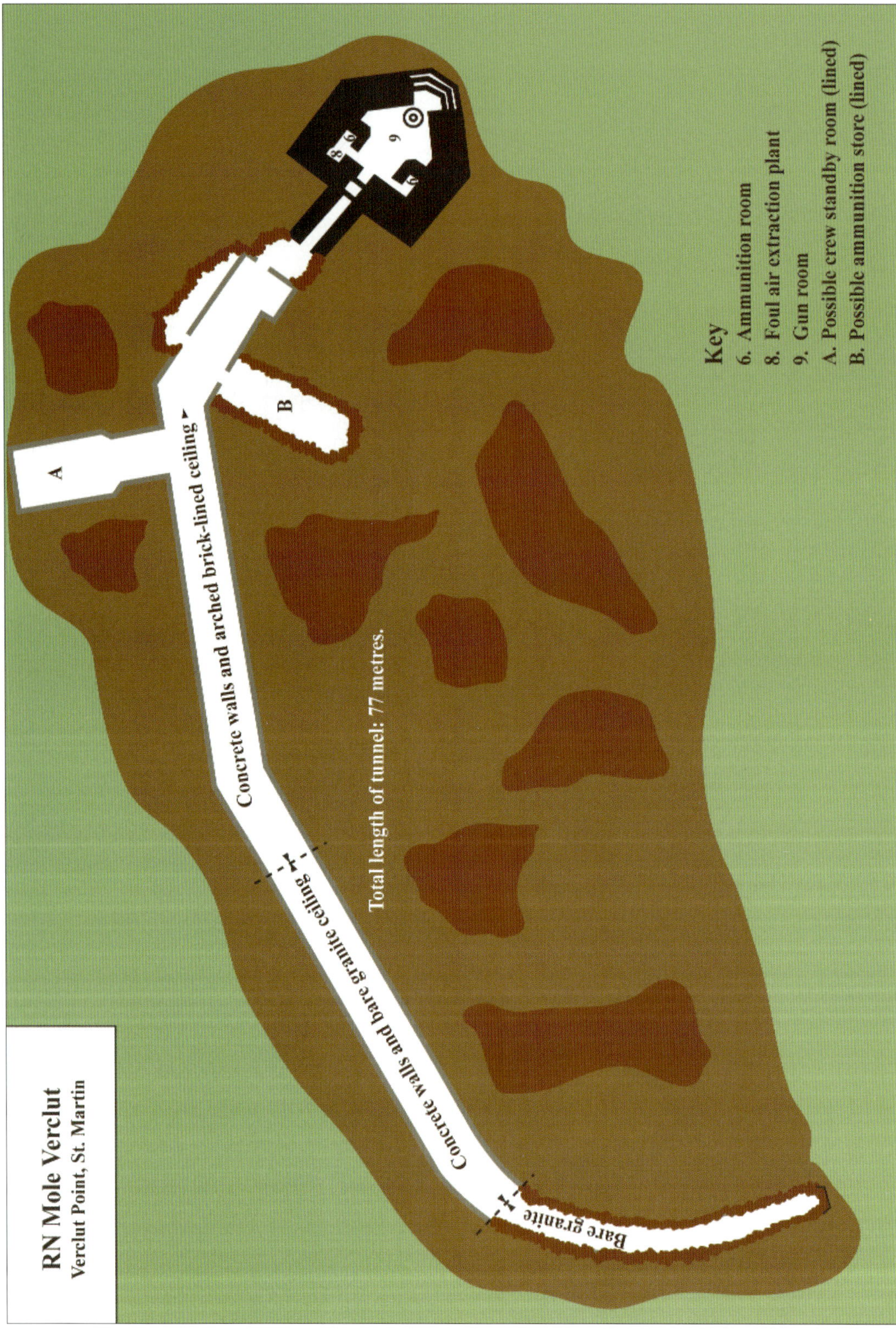

RN Mole Verclut
Verclut Point, St. Martin
Key
6. Ammunition room
8. Foul air extraction plant
9. Gun room
A. Possible crew standby room (lined)
B. Possible ammunition store (lined)
A
B
6
8
9
Concrete walls and arched brick-lined ceiling
Total length of tunnel: 77 metres.
Concrete walls and bare granite ceiling
Bare granite

Gefechtsstand

3rd Company
Machine-Gun Battalion 16
Mont Matthieu, St. Ouen

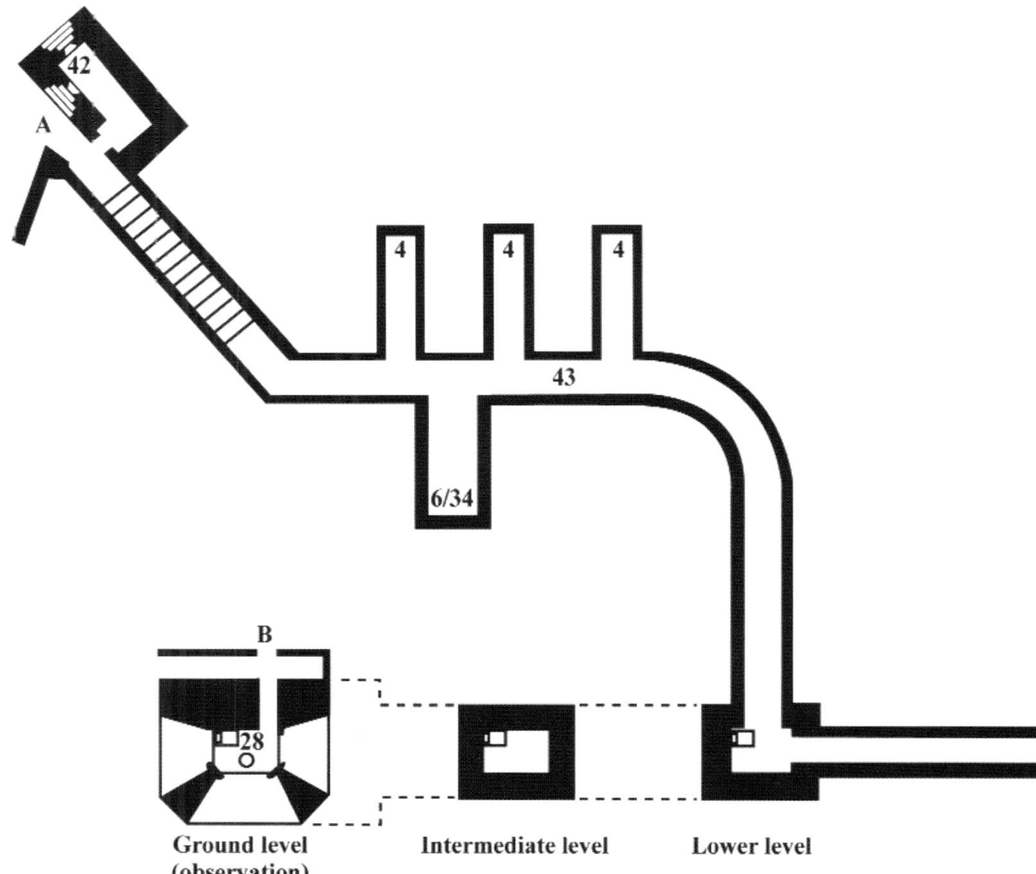

Key

4. Standby room
6. Ammunition room
28. Observation room
34. Stores
42. Machine-gun position
43. Connecting corridor

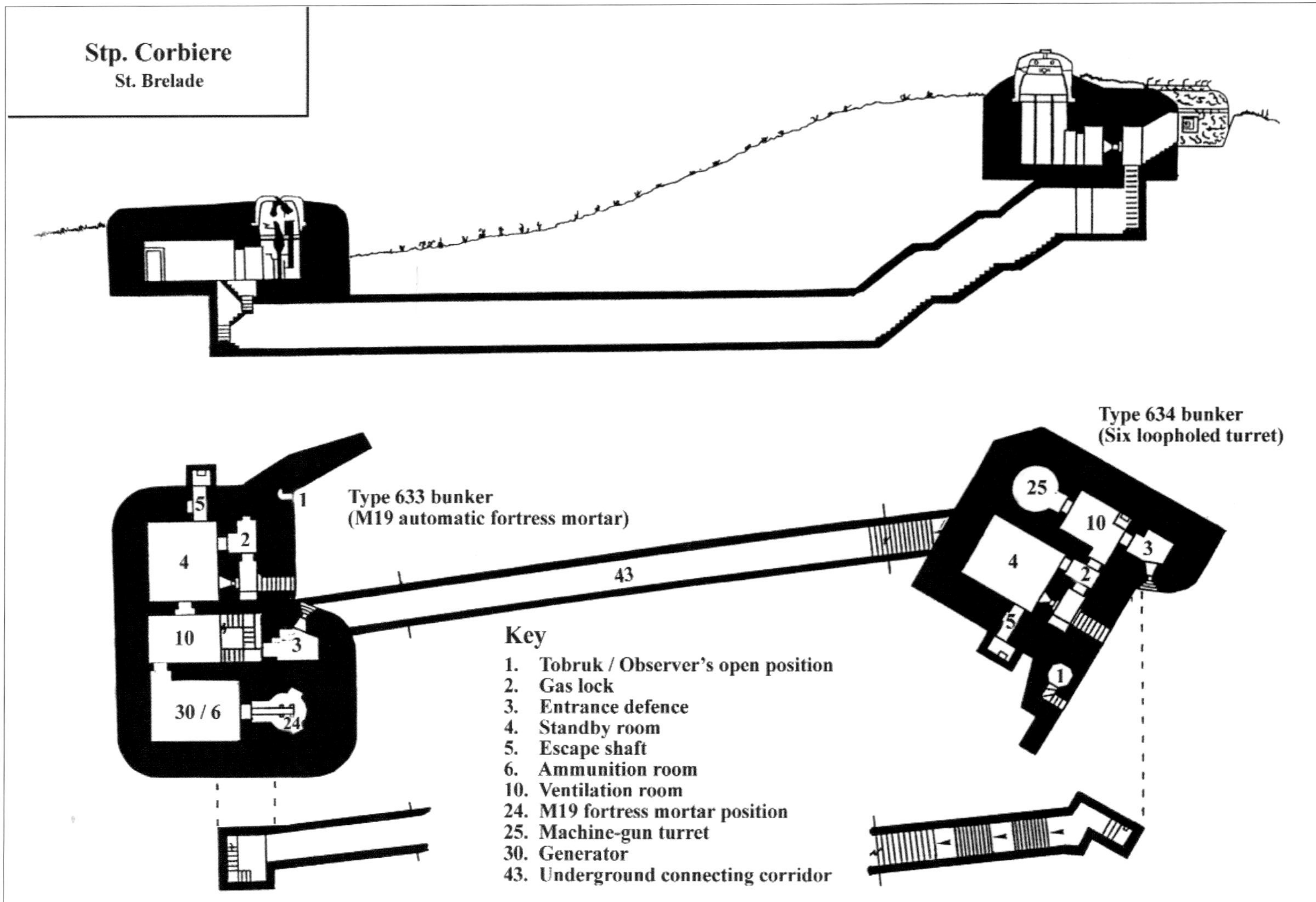
Stp. Corbiere
St. Brelade
Type 633 bunker
(M19 automatic fortress mortar)
Type 634 bunker
(Six loopholed turret)
43
Key
1. Tobruk / Observer's open position
2. Gas lock
3. Entrance defence
4. Standby room
5. Escape shaft
6. Ammunition room
10. Ventilation room
24. M19 fortress mortar position
25. Machine-gun turret
30. Generator
43. Underground connecting corridor

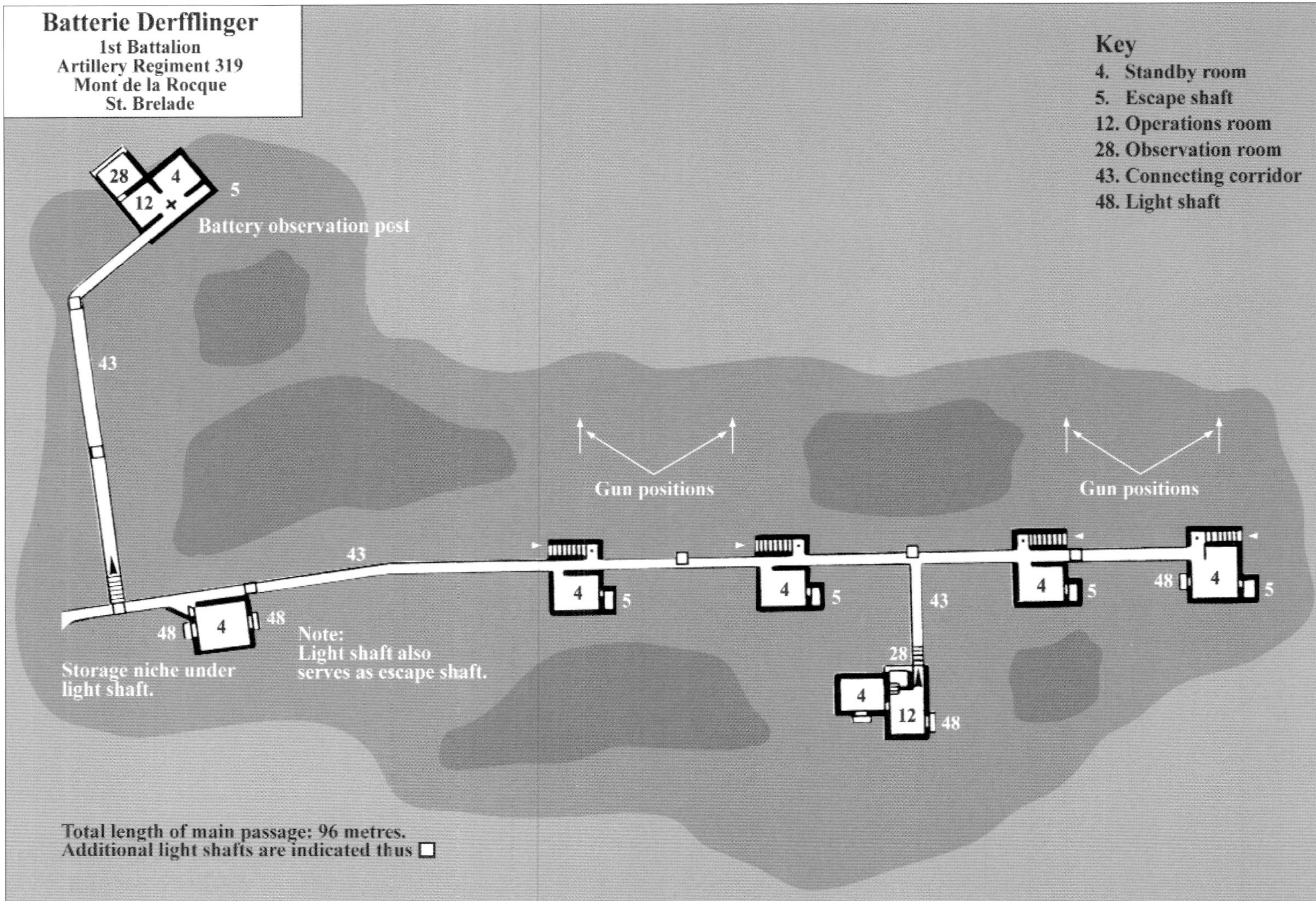

Batterie Derfflinger
1st Battalion
Artillery Regiment 319
Mont de la Rocque
St. Brelade
Key
4. Standby room
5. Escape shaft
12. Operations room
28. Observation room
43. Connecting corridor
48. Light shaft
Battery observation post
Gun positions
Gun positions
Note:
Light shaft also
serves as escape shaft.
Storage niche under
light shaft.
Total length of main passage: 96 metres.
Additional light shafts are indicated thus

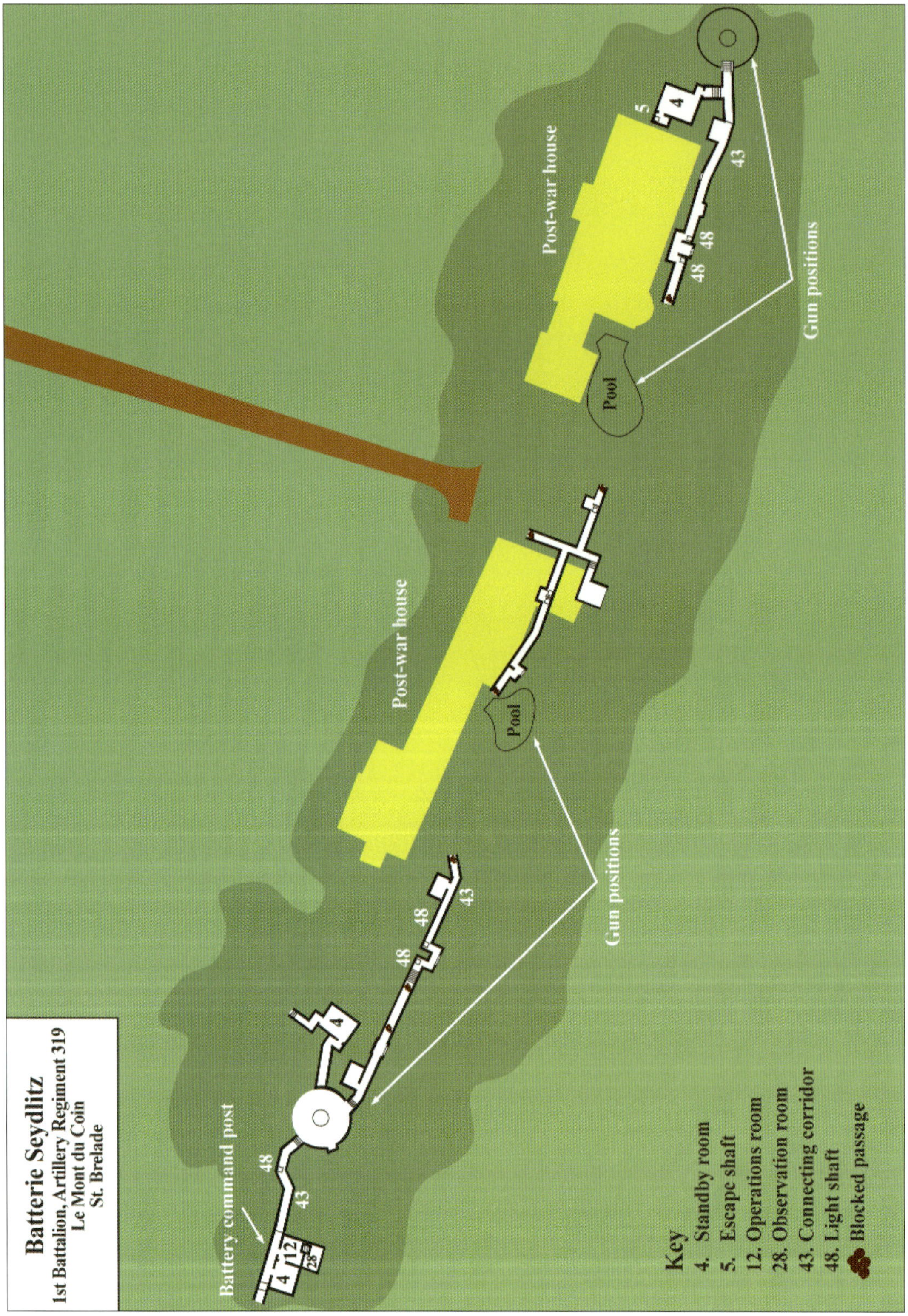

Batterie Seydlitz
1st Battalion, Artillery Regiment 319
Le Mont du Coin
St. Brelade
Battery command post
Post-war house
Post-war house
Pool
Pool
Gun positions
Gun positions
4
12
28
43
48
5
Key
4. Standby room
5. Escape shaft
12. Operations room
28. Observation room
43. Connecting corridor
48. Light shaft
Blocked passage

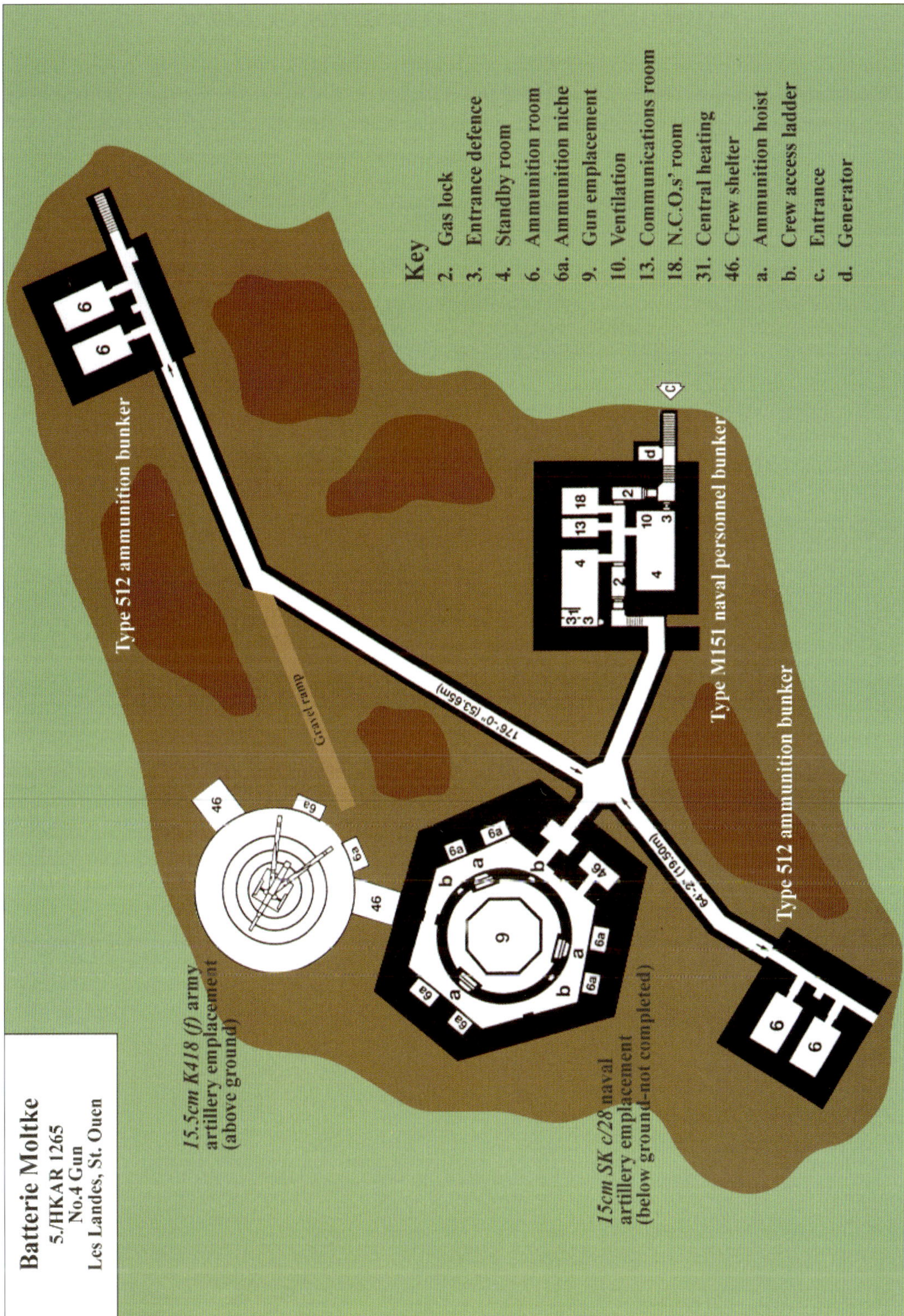

Batterie Moltke
5./HKAR 1265
No.4 Gun
Les Landes, St. Ouen
15.5cm K418 (f) army artillery emplacement (above ground)
15cm SK c/28 naval artillery emplacement (below ground-not completed)
Type 512 ammunition bunker
Type M151 naval personnel bunker
Type 512 ammunition bunker
Gravel ramp
176'-0" (53.65m)
64'-2" (19.50m)
Key
2. Gas lock
3. Entrance defence
4. Standby room
6. Ammunition room
6a. Ammunition niche
9. Gun emplacement
10. Ventilation
13. Communications room
18. N.C.O.s' room
31. Central heating
46. Crew shelter
a. Ammunition hoist
b. Crew access ladder
c. Entrance
d. Generator

Appendix IV - The Treasures of *Ho 2*

When *Ho 2* was officially re-opened in 1972, a local photographic group known as Photoquest, headed by Mr. Maurice Delanoe, visited the complex and recorded on film some of the relics that had lured collectors and others into the tunnel over the previous 26 years. Here are some of their pictures...

Removing one of the field kitchens in November, 1985. *Jersey Evening Post*

Appendix V - The 1962 Tunnel Report

Following the tragic death, through asphyxiation, of two boys in *Ho 2* on 27th May 1962, and the preliminary investigation into the incident (conducted by various military experts, and described on page 35 of this book), a report was commissioned by the States of Jersey to urgently examine the condition of all German tunnels in the Island and to recommend a course of action to prevent further incidents.

The report, which has kindly been made available by Mr. Michael Long, the States of Jersey Emergency Planning Officer, was actually in three parts:

1. Preliminary report

On 25th June 1962, Brigadier D.W. Reid, MBE, ADC, Chief Engineer, Southern Command conducted a preliminary examination of the tunnels, and produced a brief report, based solely on a visit to *Ho 2* and *Ho 8*.

Stating that the "problem of these German tunnels is a vast one," Brigadier Reid further commented:

Nobody knows how many tunnels there are, where they are and what access they have to the open. There might be five or ten miles of tunnels. The police car driver and a friend of his, with whom I spoke, knew from their schooldays far more about the tunnels and their contents than is known officially.

The Brigadier described the remaining equipment in *Ho 2* ("St. Peter's East") as a "fairy crock of gold", adding that it was a "powerful incentive to schoolboys to break into the tunnels."

Somewhat tongue-in-cheek he went on to say:

I do not consider that sealing the tunnels offers any prospect of success. Schoolboys with the adventure spirit and trained as commandos will always defeat concrete and rock given time. They are already working on Aladdin's Cave which has been re-sealed after the accident on 29 [sic] May. Sealing could in fact only be effective when all the exits and entrances are known and if they are all visited at regular intervals.

In conclusion, he stated:

... some approach should be made towards emptying the caves and towards putting up barriers and warning notices in those parts of the caves which are structurally unsafe. After emptying they should NOT be sealed because this forms a challenge to the adventurous.

As we shall see, he was later to revise this recommendation.

2. Report and survey

The Brigadier returned with a surveying unit from Southern Command, assisted by Lt. Blashford-Snell RE who, having been educated in the Island, had "local knowledge and contacts". The unit carried out a thorough inspection of all known tunnels between 2nd and 16th August 1962, presenting a further report on 19th August 1962, accompanied by plans and photographs.

The report described how contact was made with former Force 135 officers who had been involved in the liberation and clearance of the Island in 1945. It concluded that there was no evidence of chemical weapons, and "strong evidence" that no "bulk stocks" of ammunition remained. It was felt that perhaps just individual rounds and weapons may have been "mixed up with other stores".

The report identified three tunnels where miscellaneous stores were still present, "ranging from welded steel anti-tank obstacles, through barbed wire to respirator containers and empty spent ammunition drums." On the chemical side, it was observed that there was "some calcium carbide and some lead arsenate." The calcium carbide (in *Ho 2*) was considered dangerous, but more dangerous were the 1$^1/_2$ tons of lead arsenate which the States of Jersey had thoughtfully "placed" in *Ho Mole Verclut*, at St. Catherine's Breakwater, and to which access was wide open.

Of primary concern were the roof-falls, the lack of ventilation in the tunnels, and the dangers presented by open escape shafts at points where they reached the surface - located on hillsides, and often considerably overgrown.

It was the report's recommendation that such shafts be sealed. However, when the subject was raised with Messrs. Daisy Hill Real Estates, the new owners of *Ho 8* (formerly the Underground Hospital, now the Jersey War Tunnels) it caused some alarm, the Company Secretary pointing out that the shafts served an essential function as ventilators. In this instance, a compromise was reached, with the shafts being secured by grilles rather than concrete.

As for the tunnels themselves, and contrary to Brigadier Reid's earlier views on the matter, the report recommended that, wherever feasible, they be sealed by means of a 2-3 ft. thick concrete block fixed to firm rock a short distance inside, with the entrances either blown in or filled with rubble. Furthermore, it was stated that no attempt should be made to clear the contents of *Ho 2* owing to the presence of the calcium carbide.

3. Working party report

Just prior to the military inspection, the Defence Committee commissioned a working party comprising Mr. E. N. Walker (States Bomb Disposal Officer), Mr. T. Titterington (British Sub-Aqua Club), PC J. Faiers and Mr. C. Harper (States Engineer) to "gather all the factual information possible as to the number, location, condition and contents of all the tunnels in the Island as well as any other relevant information which could assist the Military Party in their investigations."

In July, 1962 letters were sent to the Parish Constables, requesting that they provide information about any known tunnels in their jurisdiction. However, the result was "disappointing", and it seems that only the Constables of St. Ouen, St. Helier and St. Clement actually replied. These enquiries yielded no additional knowledge, and the working party had to rely on observation and, as we shall see, hearsay.

The state of each complex was summarised in the working party's report dated 7th August 1962, the entry for the so-called "tunnels" at *Batterie Lothringen*, Noirmont Point, making particularly interesting reading:

A system of communicating tunnels believed to exist under the headland, probably connecting up the large bunkers and gun emplacements dotted over the headland. One entrance is known to exist, but this was blocked up soon after the Liberation and has never been re-opened. First hand report indicated that a type of tear gas was originally stored here but nothing more is known of other possible contents ...

A letter had been written to Mrs. Dixon of Noirmont Manor, asking her to confirm whether, to her knowledge, there was a connecting tunnel in the grounds of her property - approximately a quarter of a mile away!

Bearing in mind that all the fortifications on the headland were fully accessible to the public for three years after the Liberation, and that the bunkers were only sealed up in 1948, a mere 14 years prior to the report, the lack of accurate information is quite surprising.

The entry for *Ho 1* ("St. Peter's West") is also interesting:

... Built as an ammunition store and used after the Liberation as a dump for equipment of various kinds, small arms and ammunition, which has been the reason for repeated break-ins. The main part of the tunnel was used by Messrs. Val de Travers for the storage of bitumen in 1946 and afterwards was securely sealed owing to the removal of weapons and ammunition by boys. One entrance now used by the Jersey Light Car Club for various purposes which

makes nonsense of sealing. Known contents in addition to derelict vehicles includes field kitchens, trucks, empty boxes and cases, etc. Could still contain some explosives and should be considered dangerous in places.

This assessment appears to be based on hearsay, rather than fact. Note that although there is a reference to "field kitchens and trucks", there is no mention of the guns immured by Major Sargent's deliberately induced rockfalls in the northern galleries (see Appendix I).

The working party were particularly concerned by the state of *Ho 4* ("Grands Vaux Central"):

... This tunnel system was used after the war for dumping barbed wire and the whole place is practically jammed with wire. It is known, however, that explosives and live mortar bombs were also dumped here. Some have been removed and disposed of but there is still in the tunnels and under the barbed wire a quantity of TNT, bombs and probably other types of explosive. Although the Waterworks Co. endeavour to keep the entrances sealed, they have been repeatedly broken down and the tunnels entered. The removal of the stuff stored in these tunnels would be a hazardous operation and we consider the place to be extremely dangerous.

This was undoubtedly prompted by the findings of working party member, Mr. E. N. Walker, States Bomb Disposal Officer:

During inspection of this tunnel an anti-tank projectile of the German Faustpatrone 2" type was discovered among the barbed wire. This contained a charge of mixed TNT and cyclonite in good condition.

It was not possible to ascertain if others are present due to the large amount of material. However, fins and other parts were discovered which would point to others being present.

It is my opinion that these objects are dangerous and account should be taken of their presence when working in the tunnel.

The publicity surrounding the tunnel inspection resulted in several interested parties in the UK contacting the Defence Committee; one company offered its services for the sealing of all German structures; another offered to clear the tunnels for the scrap value of the artefacts; and another offered to purchase the artefacts as collectors' items. The Société Jersiaise also wrote to the Committee, requesting that they be given first refusal should any items be recovered. However, the commercial approaches were all politely declined, whilst the Société was advised that there was nothing of any interest or value.

On the recommendation of the report, and with the consent of the property owners, most of the disused tunnels were sealed or re-sealed fairly effectively using heavy duty concrete. However, as Brigadier Reid had predicted in his initial report, as long as the "Aladdin's Cave" was left untouched, the security of *Ho 2* remained an issue; with piles of helmets, respirators, ammunition boxes and field telephones still *in situ*, the tunnel continued to hold a strong attraction for schoolboys, who, undeterred by concrete and carbide, soon found their way back into the complex. This state of affairs persisted until 1972 when the States belatedly realised that the relics *were* of "interest and value", and the tunnel was finally cleared.

3. It is apparent that the problem of these German tunnels is a vast one:

(a) Nobody knows how many tunnels there are, where they are and what access they have to the open. There might be five or ten miles of tunnels. The police car driver and a friend of his, with whom I spoke, knew from their school-days far more about the tunnels and their contents than is known officially.

(b) No list of equipment stored in the tunnels is available. It is clear that there is comparatively little danger of CW substances or of explosives although there may be some danger of tear gas which was used as a training expedient.

(c) Many of the tunnels are in a potentially dangerous state, the uncompleted portions have been supported on timber props which have now rotted and there is clear evidence of roof falls.

(d) There are constant stories of a good supply of ammunition and weapons being somewhere stored away. This is the equivalent of the "fairy crock of gold" and is a powerful incentive to schoolboys to break into the tunnels.

4. I do not consider that sealing the tunnels offers any prospect of success. Schoolboys with the adventure spirit and trained as commandos will always defeat concrete and rock given time. They are already working in Aladdin's Cave which has been re-sealed after the accident on 29 May. Sealing could in fact only be effective when all the exits and entrances are known and if they are all visited at regular intervals.

5. The problem of clearing the caves is a formidable one, but how formidable is impossible as yet to assess. The problem is aggravated by the dangerous condition of some parts of the caves. If they were to be emptied however, the chief incentive to exploration would be removed.

Fig. 123 - An extract from Brigadier Reid's preliminary report dated 25th June 1962 wherein *Ho 2* is described as an "Aladdin's Cave". Note that the date of the tragedy is erroneously referred to as 29th instead of 27th May. *Courtesy Michael Long*

JdeF/VB.

Telephone: Central 33201, Ext. 273.

All communications should be addressed to the Greffier of the States.

STATES' GREFFE,
JERSEY.

Our Ref. 192(34)

Your Ref.

2nd July, 1962.

Dear Sir,

I have been asked by the Acting President of the Defence Committee to inform you that following the recent accident which occurred in the ex-German tunnel in St. Peter's Valley, arrangements are being made with Brigadier D. W. Reid, M.B.E., A.D.C., Chief Engineer, Southern Command, to dispatch a small reconnaissance party to the Island in the near future to draw up reasonably accurate plans of the layout of all ex-German tunnels, with particular reference to all exits, entrances and other means of access so that some course of action may be decided upon to improve their safety.

Your assistance and the assistance of your police officers would be particularly valuable in that a preliminary working party has been set up to collate as much local knowledge as possible of the whereabouts and contents of ex-German tunnels in the Island before the arrival of the recce. party. It would be greatly appreciated therefore, if you could pass on any relevant information of this nature to this office (a form is attached for this purpose) if possible during the course of the next week. I would however, stress that information is required only upon tunnels or suspected dumps or caches of ex-German equipment and not on what might be termed strong points or bunkers of which a considerable knowledge is already held by the States' Engineer's Department.

Yours faithfully,

Deputy Greffier of the States.

This letter sent to all Constables.

Fig. 124 - Letter sent to the Constables by the Greffier of the States on 2nd July 1962, requesting information about the "whereabouts and contents of the ex-German tunnels". ***Courtesy Michael Long***

192(34)

Your ref: JdeF/VB.
192(34)

TELEPHONE: WEST 119

LA SALLE PAROISSIALE,
ST. OUEN,
JERSEY.

PARISH HALL,
ST. OUEN,
JERSEY.

9th. July, 1962.

STATES GREFFE
REGISTERED
10 JUL 1962
JERSEY

The Greffier of the States,
States' Greffe,
ST. HELIER, JERSEY.

Dear Sir,

Although there are, of course, many bunkers and other such ex-German defence works of various kinds in the Parish of St. Ouen, a number of them in a dangerous condition, I do not know of any such which might contain ammunition or equipment. Children would be the first to find out these things but to the best of my knowledge, and that of the other Police officers of the Parish, none has come to light. This does not preclude there being ammunition or equipment in some of these constructions, for few of the more complicated underground systems can have been explored by local people. I believe that there might have been some sort of storage tunnel connecting with the bunker opening out on to Mont Matthieu opposite La Rocque Onvoy, but Mr. E.C.G. Corneliusen, under whose property the bunker is, would be able to tell you more about this. It would seem that the equipment and ammunition found in the tunnels off St. Peter's Valley were cleared out from the defence works all over the Island, and this was probably the case at St. Ouen.

Yours faithfully,

E.W. Vautier,
Connêtable.

Fig. 125 - One of the few responses to the Greffier's request – this from the Constable of St. Ouen.
Courtesy Michael Long

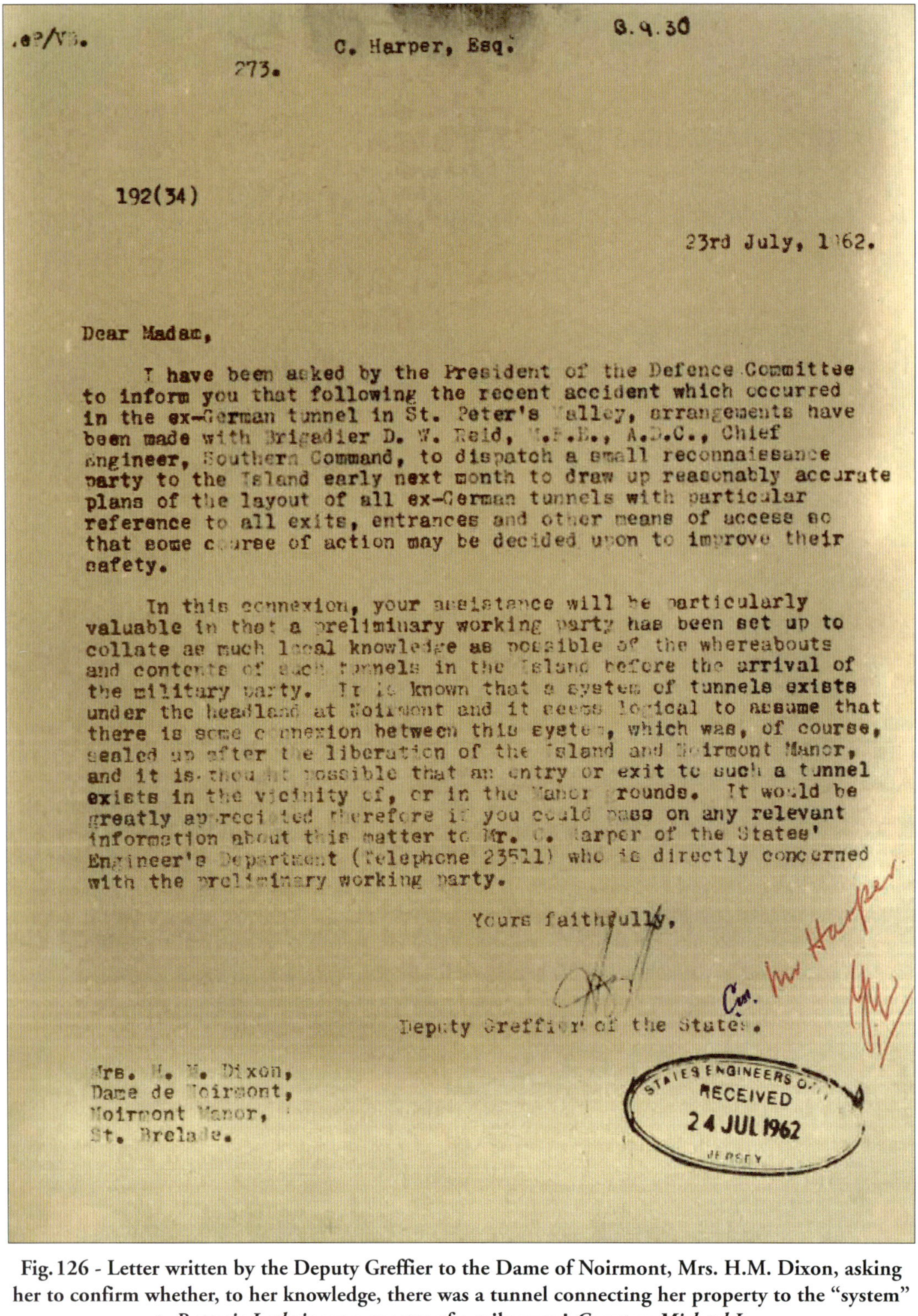

.e?/V?. C. Harper, Esq. 8.9.30

273.

192(34)

23rd July, 1962.

Dear Madam,

I have been asked by the President of the Defence Committee to inform you that following the recent accident which occurred in the ex-German tunnel in St. Peter's Valley, arrangements have been made with Brigadier D. W. Reid, O.B.E., A.D.C., Chief Engineer, Southern Command, to dispatch a small reconnaissance party to the Island early next month to draw up reasonably accurate plans of the layout of all ex-German tunnels with particular reference to all exits, entrances and other means of access so that some course of action may be decided upon to improve their safety.

In this connexion, your assistance will be particularly valuable in that a preliminary working party has been set up to collate as much local knowledge as possible of the whereabouts and contents of such tunnels in the Island before the arrival of the military party. It is known that a system of tunnels exists under the headland at Noirmont and it seems logical to assume that there is some connexion between this system, which was, of course, sealed up after the liberation of the Island and Noirmont Manor, and it is thought possible that an entry or exit to such a tunnel exists in the vicinity of, or in the Manor grounds. It would be greatly appreciated therefore if you could pass on any relevant information about this matter to Mr. C. Harper of the States' Engineer's Department (Telephone 23511) who is directly concerned with the preliminary working party.

Yours faithfully,

Deputy Greffier of the States.

Co. Mr Harper

Mrs. H. M. Dixon,
Dame de Noirmont,
Noirmont Manor,
St. Brelade.

STATES ENGINEERS O.
RECEIVED
24 JUL 1962
JERSEY

Fig. 126 - Letter written by the Deputy Greffier to the Dame of Noirmont, Mrs. H.M. Dixon, asking her to confirm whether, to her knowledge, there was a tunnel connecting her property to the "system" at *Batterie Lothringen* a quarter of a mile away! *Courtesy Michael Long*

Fig. 127 - A member of the surveying unit from Southern Command outside the pedestrian entrance to *Ho 1*, August, 1962. *John Blashford-Snell, Courtesy Michael Long*

Fig. 128 - Examining the "Aladdin's Cave" in *Ho 2*.
John Blashford-Snell, Courtesy Michael Long

Fig. 129 - The lower (southern) entrance to *Ho15* with pit-props still in position.
John Blashford-Snell, Courtesy Michael Long

Fig. 130 - The casemate bunker fronting the tunnel complex at *Ho Mole Verclut* as it appeared in August, 1962. Used by the States to store 1½ tons of lead arsenate, the complex was all too easily accessible. *John Blashford-Snell, Courtesy Michael Long*

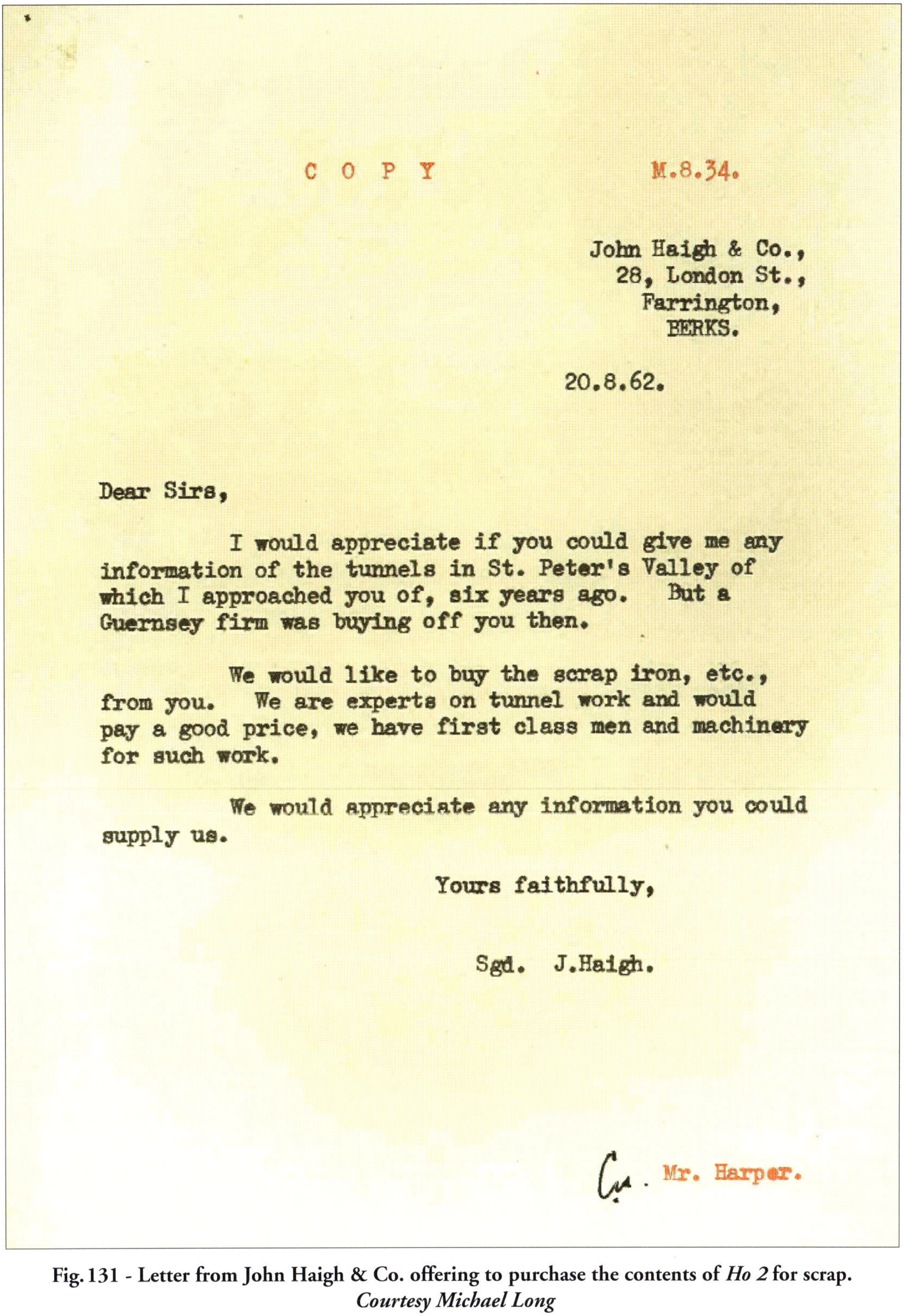
C O P Y M.8.34.

John Haigh & Co.,
28, London St.,
Farrington,
BERKS.

20.8.62.

Dear Sirs,

I would appreciate if you could give me any information of the tunnels in St. Peter's Valley of which I approached you of, six years ago. But a Guernsey firm was buying off you then.

We would like to buy the scrap iron, etc., from you. We are experts on tunnel work and would pay a good price, we have first class men and machinery for such work.

We would appreciate any information you could supply us.

Yours faithfully,

Sgd. J.Haigh.

Cu. Mr. Harper.

Fig. 131 - Letter from John Haigh & Co. offering to purchase the contents of *Ho 2* for scrap.
Courtesy Michael Long

JdeF/VB.

273.

C. Harper, Esq.

STATES ENGINEERS OFFICE RECEIVED 13 SEP 1967 JERSEY

192(34)

12th September, 1962.

Dear Sir,

The President of the Defence Committee has asked me to refer to your letter dated 9th August, 1962, requesting articles of uniform or equipment, which might be retrieved as a result of the examination of the ex-German tunnels and which could be placed in the German Occupation Museum, or the Grounds at Hougue Bie.

Unfortunately, whilst the press seems to have created the impression that considerable stores have been unearthed, the military survey party has not found anything of interest in retrievable condition. Nevertheless your request will be borne in mind.

Yours faithfully,

J. E. F. DE FAYE

Secretary,
Defence Committee.

G. C. H. Le Cocq, Esq.,
Secretary,
Société Jersiaise,
The Museum,
9, Pier Road,
St. Helier.

Fig. 132 - Letter to the Secretary of the Société Jersiaise from the Secretary of the Defence Committee advising that the military survey party had "not found anything of interest in retrievable condition". ***Courtesy Michael Long***

Figs.133 & 134 - 'Before' and 'after' photographs showing the sealing of one of the access points to the rear galleries of *Ho 1*. The vehicles belonged to the Jersey Light Car Club. ***Courtesy Michael Long***

Appendix VI - Gallery

Jersey's German tunnels – striking images from a new generation of photographers.

Ho 1 **Tony Pike**

Ho 1 **Jimmy Gray @UnseenJersey.com**

Ho 1 **Jimmy Gray @UnseenJersey.com**

Ho 1 **Si Prosser @UnseenJersey.com**

Ho 1 **Si Prosser @UnseenJersey.com**

Ho 2 **Steve Powell**

Ho 2 **Steve Powell**

Ho 2 **Steve Powell**

Ho 2 **Steve Powell**

Ho 2 **Steve Powell**

Ho 2 **Steve Powell**

Ho 4 **Neil Walker**

Ho 4 **Neil Walker**

Ho 5 **Si Prosser @UnseenJersey.com**

Ho 8 **Jimmy Gray @UnseenJersey.com**

Ho 13 **Jimmy Gray @UnseenJersey.com**

Ho 13 **Si Prosser @UnseenJersey.com**

Ho 19 **Jimmy Gray @UnseenJersey.com**